HOW TO GET HAPPIER
- and why you should try to

Also by Elizabeth Power

Getting the Fat Out Of Your Head
(so it stays off your body!)

If Change Is All There Is, Choice Is All You've Got

Managing Our Selves: Building A Community of Caring

Managing Our Selves: God In Our Midst

The ASk Video Series: Associative Skills:
Taking Charge of Change
The Trouble with Feelings
Boundaries Precious Boundaries

www.GettingHappier.com

www.ElizabethPower.com

www.epowerandassociates.com

How to **Get Happier**

—and why you should try to!

by

Elizabeth Power

www.GettingHappier.com

Graphics by Poole Advertising

Published by Big Happy Press

www.GettingHappier.com

ISBN 1-883307-08-2

ISBN 978-1-883307-08-0

First edition, February 2009

Second edition, March 2011

Inspiration

The inspiration for this book spans 50 plus years, thousands of people who were the participants in my efforts to get happier, and the many who were cast aside or who cast me aside as I thrashed out of my husk and into life.

I thank you profoundly for what you each helped me learn.

May the patience you exhibited, the truth that you told, the hopes that you held be fulfilled—from North Carolina to New York, from Tennessee to California, all around the world—it was your efforts that plowed the ground and sowed the seeds that blossomed into this work.

This book is for the gamut of people from seekers of self-development to folks who are just tired of having their past run their lives or who feel stuck in their present.

It's also for people who know that they're happy and recognize they can always get happier, or maybe influence someone else they meet along the way.

Happiness. I'm all for it,

Elizabeth Power

My cat Charlie reigns.

Poole Advertising rules.

Sally Poole rocks.

Lisa Novinger rocks.

Adrianna Molina double rocks.

All my readers—Annita Jones, Mike Uretsky, Barbara Boat, Nancy Brookshire, Joyce Bender, Steve Gold, Ann Hart, Pam Pannell—rock for taking time to read this in the rough.

My Nashville peeps for their support for the second edition. You know who you are.

Table of Content

What if—every day—you just got a little happier? Not a lot, not all at once.

Adding contentment on contentment to the excitement of possibility?

Chapter One:
When Life Slings You Like a Lemon in A Blender

The first twenty years.

I was born, according to my Vedic astrologer friend, in a whole heap of trouble. Rahu was on top of Rahu on top of Rahu the first twenty years of my life.

While I really can't tell you much about what that means from his world, I can tell you from mine that life exerted an exceptionally strong negative vacuum those first two decades. Strong enough it probably could have picked up a cannon ball and held on to it for a very, very long time.

Rahu's vacuum makes a "strong sucking sound" for the first twenty years

My evangelical friends shrug and talk about generational curses, my liberal friends talk about family dysfunction. It doesn't matter which world view you live with, the end result was all the same: a really hard time. No details needed, make them up, embellish them, and then keep on going. We'll cover that spiritual stuff later.

There were a lot of very good things that happened, a lot of learning that did in fact stand me in good stead.

When Life Slings You Like a Lemon in A Blender

Classical art, literature and music. Growing up spending a lot of time outside. Lots of cousins around.

A mama determined her children wouldn't grow up and be stuck in the edge of Appalachia. Reading from the age of five—well, I don't know. The cost of a pound of paper to read in two hours is steep.

Practice makes perfect!

Still yet, the making of a lunatic was the warp and woof of the fabric of those years. Moving so often before I was two that I really only feel comfortable with a packed bag somewhere near by. Daddy's death before I was two and a half.

Learning to zip right out of my body—and my mind. St. Vitus' dance and weeks on Phenobarbital choreographing the dancing. Bad knees (surgery about six times on each one). A very sad and stressed Mama who did her best and was, well, more than a little shut down.

I think I knew that old saw "My feet hurt and I don't even love Jesus anymore" before it was written. We just never quite fit in.

Throw in the general dysfunction you're likely to find anywhere, about four or five of the Adverse Childhood experiences in Felliti's study (don't you just love his name?) and it's just a miracle I'm here.

So far.

That second twenty years?

Oh mercy. The attitude I developed during those first twenty was just getting warmed up. I had learned crazy but good.

I was intense, sarcastic, peripatetic (look it up), chronically PO'd, hateful, determined everyone else was wrong (and they were) and that I was right (and I was).

If I couldn't have Happy, I'd hate it instead. That'd show Happy a thing or two!

If bizarre was within twenty miles I could smell it in the air and was pulled towards it like it was a supermagnet. That book is a collection of weird-grams!

I'd started practicing unhappy in my teens, about the time I left home, and I got reallllll good at it. Fact of the matter is that I practiced creating unhappy a lot because I knew it so well.

I dug a big old deep Unhappy hole and piled all the garbage I'd hung on to in it. By now it was great compost, nice and warm and smelly. Perfect. I jumped in and stayed.

When Life Slings You Like a Lemon in A Blender

I lived in, clung to, and fertilized my big old Unhappy Hole on a regular basis. What got planted for me in the first twenty I tended and weeded and fed in the second twenty.

Had a great crop, a bountiful harvest of Unhappy.

I was in my element in that big old Unhappy Lot, making my garden of misery better and better every chance I could. Let me tell you, I'd learned some great tricks and techniques.

Getting Happier is a good investment in your Unhappy Hole

Except that these little glimpses of Happy kept cropping up. I remember seeing them when I was just a child, and trying to grab on to them.

Other people acted like they had Happy in their lives and I wanted it, but couldn't get it. I'd have a little smell of it, tentatively take a little sip, and off it would go. Vanished. Gone into thin air.

I got so mad at the Happy disappearing I began to treat it like a weed, chopping it out of my life every chance I got. If I couldn't have it, I'd hate it instead. That'd show Happy a thing or two.

This twenty?

Finally. I began to change crops. I decided I'd hated Happy long enough, and that as a free, choice-making citizen of the world's showcase for democracy, I could choose to be happy. I could will it into my life, and be happy.

Well, at least more and more so. Happy, that is. OK, Happier. As for the willing to be, about all I did was bend and break my will a couple of times. Practice little tiny choices over and over instead. It's easier.

And I am. Happier, that is.

It's interesting—I'm at the 15 year point of the third 20, and what I've noticed is this: getting happier is a good thing. It's a good investment in your big old Unhappy Hole, whatever size it is.

I believe you can get happier too, no matter how healthy or horrific your childhood, functional or dysfunctional your family, combat-impacted your relationship, how otherwise fouled up you have become—or aren't.

I didn't say perfect, living in complete and total ecstasy—I said happier.

And yes, I said getting happier is

a good investment in your big old Unhappy Hole—and I promise that by the time you've read the whole book you'll know why. If you don't, give me a holler.

Here are a couple of hints about that, because I know you're just waiting with bated breath to know the basis for such an outrageous statement:

- The more you strengthen Happy, the better able you are to recognize the home of Unhappy.
- The better you are at recognizing that big old Unhappy Hole, the earlier you'll catch it.
- The earlier you catch it, the more choice you have about whether or not to climb in.

About getting slung around like a lemon in a blender? Well, if the economy and world events **haven't** made you feel that way even just a little bit lately I'd say check in with your nearest trusted mental health professional.

Most of us are holding our breath waiting for the blender to stop. If it's already stopped, we're just trying to pick up the pieces and go on with making lemonade.

When Life Slings You Like a Lemon in A Blender

In either case, hiking up your Happy will make it easier to get through it all. Here's the bottom line:

Life will get worse. Life will get better.

You can **always** get a little happier.

You'll always have a choice, if abut nothing else, how you feel. When you fall in love with "choice" you're on your way.

Some people frame "falling in love with choice" as being a "control freak." Is it really?

If I'm in love with choice, it's about the choices I see, feel, and experience. If I'm a "control freak," that seems to be more about the choices I want someone else to make.

So if life seems to be slinging you like a lemon in a blender, look at your choices. You can:

- Learn to love the ride
- Jam the blades
- Wait for it to stop
- Lean and tip it over
- Consider it a form of trance dance.

Whatever you choose, make sure it helps you hike up your Happy.

Oh that every woman with child
feels only contentment, joy, plenty and peace!

Oh that every child born
knew these in their bones, in their hearts,
in their homes.

That gratitude would fill the cosmos with light.

Chapter Two: First Things First

How'd you Learn Happy?

You know the types: Miss Cheery Denial, whose life is a shambles and she loves it (but doesn't know it!); Vicky (or Victor) the Professional Victim, delighting in every opportunity to let what is happening be someone else's fault. To revel in their own victimization and how bad things always seem to happen to them (and no one else).

We're all a little nuts, right?

You can clearly see how they set themselves up for the crap every time. Martina Martyriliva, whose body is screaming the results of the sacrifice but whose mouth puts out "I'm fine!" (I think I saw her self-flagellating in the steam room at the Y last week).

There's a whole slew more of them: Tawanna the Trauma Queen and her sister Dierde the Drama Queen. So close they're almost twins. Serella the Serial Spouse. Abila the Abusive Aholle, and Vlad the Violent. I won't bore you with the entire alliterative alphabet (but I could).

First Things First

There's probably a little of each of those wackos in all of us, mixed in with our own unique blend of craziness. OK, we're a lot more like some of them than we want to admit. And we can sure see it in everyone else.

We can almost always spot the telephone pole someone is dangling from a lot more easily than we can see the one we're hanging on. Pole, that is.

We are now who we were when we were four—and we learned that from our Big People...who learned it from their Big People!

We can see the wires that threaten electrocution, the broken ones arcing on the ground. We can see the craft that crashed—maybe it was a champagne hot air balloon flight—and put them there. Right there, on the wires.

We think we know every poor decision they made that put them there. We're pretty sure we can sort out the bad judgments from the good, and we **know** we would never do that.

What do they—that crowd—see when they look at us? Are we willing to see it in ourselves? Probably not.

We're usually as busy as three cats—one looking, one digging, and one covering up—trying to keep things going. We're usually pretty hard pressed to step back, look at our own lives, and see them as a landscape of patterns. Who can afford to?

It seems like there are generations and groups of people who learn Unhappy as a lifestyle, and yes, I know that genetics play a big role.

Nonetheless, if hooking up and getting connected with the people that change your didee and give you your bottle and bankie is a key, there are some known patterns that can make that less likely to succeed.

You learn whatever you know of Happy—and Unhappy—from the big people in your life. If the big people consider what almost every one else would call deep depression "happy" the bar is set pretty low.

If their idea of kindness or entertainment is what others call senseless violence, your bars will be set at very different angles when it comes to what constitutes Happy and Unhappy.

In other words, from the beginning of your life until you learn and do something else, your definition of Happy, what it looks and acts like, is someone else's.

Fodder for the Unhappy Hole

Think about my big old Unhappy Hole. It was a gully with red clay banks that was so deep I could barely see daylight. When the cows wandered by in the pasture up above, sometimes what they left behind dribbled down.

I spent so much time in my Unhappy Hole that I'd taken my arm chair, cooler, broke-down TV and plants in there. And my plants were stickery, thorny, bitter tough rooted things. I reveled in cockle burrs, Spanish nettles, and tough old cactus with sharp spines. I could grow them to near-perfection. In large quantity. At record speed.

The only box I ever got into? Unhappy.

It was a hole filled with unhappiness that I couldn't climb out of, even though it was actually a gully with one end open. I couldn't see that open end for all the misery I packed in there with me, focused on, and nurtured.

Do you have an Unhappy Hole? What does **your** Unhappy Hole look like? What are you taking in there with you to keep it up? How often do you climb down in it?

One way to figure out how you might be doing on the Happy scale is to look at events that most people know usually dig the Unhappy Hole deeper.

"Most people" include the majority of the folks who are not (currently) hospitalized for mental illness, and people whose opinion I respect because they appear to plant, choose, and harvest more genuine Happy than others do. Why pick them?

Well, it's like this. Even though I know full well that their garden in life has plants they might call weeds, their gardens look pretty good to me.

They seem to be well-liked, fit in when they want or need to, can see the beauty and pleasure in life without alcohol or drugs as their filter, and their health seems good. Where they are now looks like Happy to me.

So back to the events. You know the names of most of those events, whether or not you have the fruits and seeds from them. Whether or not you can pack them into your personal garden and fertilize that Unhappy Hole with them.

Bless Mama—she did the very best she could! (So did yours.)

Now this is the difference.

If they happened, whether or not you think they affected you in any way, they're in your garden.

Simple as that. Whether my daddy's death impacted me or not, I couldn't "undie" him. That one was, and is, in my garden.

All those moves before he died, all eight gazillion of them? Transiency is in there too.

I consider it a miracle that I've been in the same city since 1979, except for four years, and had the same mailing address most of the time. Of course, I changed residences pretty often, and now am working to beat the average home buyer's length of stay in one home (three years these days). I'd like to be here a while.

Back to those moves—step in my mama's shoes for a few minutes. The man of her life was a salesman, on the road all the time, emotionally and physically unavailable just because he was gone. She had one and then two small children, and he up and got sick—really sick—when the littlest, yours truly, was still really little.

What did she have left over to give? Where were her resources? How could she even have time to make friends? What support would have been available to her?

She didn't get a fair shake, and didn't have one to give. She gave the best she could, did the best she could with what she had. Then again, what they say where I come from is "Fair's what you take your pig to!"

That's in my garden, too, (not the pig) that chronic disruption and chaos—it's just <u>there</u>. It's up to me what I did, do, and will do with it when it turns ugly.

By the way, think about how often parents relocate for work, or have changed caregivers for their very young children.

Or parents who have chronic illness, or who are overwhelmed by demands made on their lives. Their lives look like patches of thistle plants, full of stickers and prickly spines.

See, a weed is only a weed when it's a plant where you want another one to be. The clippings from that St. Augustine grass I swear at while spending entirely too much time trying to yank it out of the ground becomes some very good compost under some circumstances.

A weed is only a weed when it's a plant whose place is at odds with what you want

And that dandelion? The greens it grows are fabulous on salads, and the birds love the seeds. The children love to blow the dried flower. And this dandelion we call... a weed.

Here's the truth: A weed is only a weed when it's a plant in the way of something else, or when it's serving some purpose at odds with what you intend. Sometimes that weed is a godsend if you step on the other side of it and notice how it can be of benefit. Artichokes, by the way, are a form of the thistle plant.

First Things First

Common sense trumps science: before birth, your mother shares everything (yes) with you.

Think about it: whatever went through your mother coursed through you. Happy mom? Unhappy... stressed... defeated mom? Those little patterns of chemicals and hormones—oh yes.

Whatever adjustments they make are made, ah, um, to your DNA,

and to ever pattern you learn in utero. And you have no influence over them before you're born. None. It really is all about your parents BB (that's Before Birth).

Curious? Look at the questions on the next page. Those are the kinds of questions to ask yourself, or if you're brave enough, to ask other folks about.

Remember, everyone is obligated to some degree to play the stories in one direction or another, so take all of what you hear with a little grain of salt!

You may be amazed at what you hear.

And for mercy's sake, there's no relationship to science here. None—it's all just a matter of thinking. I've heard tell there's research about it, but haven't read it. Wouldn't understand it if I did.

No studies have been done, no animals involved (let alone harmed) and these are nothing more than the observations of a reluctant sage in the making.

Curious questions:

- What was going on in your family, especially your mother when you were conceived (now that's a question! It's about her life, not the sex, OK?)?
- Was there enough money to live on or did your parents have concerns about making ends meet?
- Was there delight or shame around your conception? (Of course, you may not have the intimate details of this!)
- Were you welcomed or did you feel as if you were viewed by some as another burden?
- Were both your father and mother present or only your mother before you were born and the first few years?
- Were they settled, content and in love with each other or was the relationship in trouble?
- How much partying, drinking and drugging was going on (that you know of)?

Baby see, baby do—oops!

Baby see, baby adjust to please the Other (gotta survive—there's food out there!)

An interesting thing happens in the first minutes, hours, days, weeks once we're outside the womb. After being exposed to a whole new, dry, cold, very loud, and probably pretty terrifying environment, we begin to connect with the people outside.

First Things First

It's got to be a real shock.

Can you imagine seeing faces for the first time? Going from the warm wet interior to the bright exterior with shapes? How cold it would be?

And for the first time ever we are disconnected from the life line? The first one we start hooking up with is, hopefully, our mother. We have to connect—or hook up emotionally in a way that pleases her—if we want to survive.

If we're lucky, she looks at us lovingly, holds us in her arms, feels warm feelings, and looks us over with great care.

Her gaze is strong, direct, embracing, and oxytocin, the bonding or "tending and befriending" hormone, runs high.

That ooey-gooey feeling of love and delight in us, happiness at our being pours out of her like honey. We send it right back. It's how we begin the process of becoming human. We learn through observing, imitation, the results of our efforts.

Look these questions over. How would you answer them?

- Any chance you were premature?
- Were you separated from your birth mother when you were little (work, illness, deployment, separation,

divorce and other causes) or was your mom present in your life everyday, most of the day?

- Was your mother "in touch," vibrant, positive, smiling, easily pleased?
- When someone wanted to talk about something difficult, could she—without getting "weird," or all worked up?
- If a child fell, or a pet was hurt, or someone was upset, did she go to assist, allowing emotions as well as taking action to tend injury?
- If your mom or caregiver worked, was there enough of her left after work to be available to her family or did she work at least two jobs (what she got paid for, and being mother/wife)?
- Did she read to you? Play with you acting **your** age (not hers)?
- Think about your father in terms of these questions—any big difference? Any big similarities?

From the womb to the tomb, we learn how to be human

What I'm getting at is that from the time we exit the womb until we end up in the tomb, we are learning how to become human beings. And amazing things happen in those first few years. Simply amazing.

We learn if we can be visible to others when we are in distress, if our distress and happiness matter, if we can depend on others to be there for us when we're in distress, what we can afford to let happen (or let be known).

We learn whether or not we can be seen, or heard, or present in our own lives. We learn how safe the world is, and what we can expect from it.

Is the world safe?

Whatever is going for the people around us goes on for us, whatever we learn is what they show us. We mirror whatever is required to make sure we survive with the least risk possible.

And that becomes the level at which our "normal" settles. From the moment that this "normal" becomes our level, we spend the rest of our lives trying to maintain it, ensure it, make sure everything else lines up with it, and adjust it based on what happens in our lives.

When we recognize some other level of normal is more important to us, we shift our "normal"—the level, the texture, how it looks, what challenges it, and how we handle those challenges.

Do the people around you relish violence whether on TV or in person? Do they love the drama of trauma? Is acting like "bad" is "good" the normal? Just how did the seeds planted in your early life look?

Remember, if you call a big old tomato plant a weed, you'll pull it up, chop it out, or kill it off. It just depends on what you learn—early on—is "normal."

And the bad news? If you think becoming your mother (or father) is something you don't want to do, it's usually unavoidable. Not becoming like them is like rolling uphill: it takes a lot of effort!

Almost everyone wakes up and does the best they are able to do—that is, few people actually plan how to screw things up!

Now, it doesn't require any "make wrongs" where you devote time and attention to how awful they were and it doesn't require making them gods and goddesses who can do no wrong.

It only takes recognizing that they did—just as you do—the best they could. In your world if you find something you'd like to experience differently, you can.

Yes. You can.

Do you actually wake up some mornings and think "I believe I will get up and just screw this day up royally for the heck of it!"?

Or somewhere in the middle of a rough day commit to "What a day! I'm going to make like a spider monkey jacked up on an energy drink, cause a little chaos and break everything I touch. This is going to be good."

I don't think so. And aside from the usual exceptions—maybe two of every hundred people—the people who raised us didn't either.

Tiny, those old early raising up issues, right? Right. Um, no.

They. Are. Huge.

Trying to please the Big People can keep babies as busy as three cats...

Babies and toddlers and little kids, especially the babies who haven't acquired or developed language and can't ask for what they want using words, can't survive without the Big People.

Everything Little People do is about having to depend on Big People for life. Crying gets me hurt? I'll be quiet.

Or somewhere in the middle of a rough day commit to "What a day! I'm going to make like a spider monkey jacked up on go juice."

Having needs upsets the milk factory? I won't have needs. They get angry and their faces turn black when I cry? I won't cry.

I feel cold and wet—they come change my diaper, look at me, smile at me, hold me—I can experience uncomfortable physical events without fear.

Imagine how cold a wet diaper could be when you just spent nine months in total warmth.

How the closest thing to a return to that closeness and comfort is being held, skin-to-skin, cuddled in warmth.

The difference is in how it feels to experience "because it's my job" and "because I love you and want the best for you, I am here to protect and keep you safe."

Conception doesn't come with a warning light

This is the difference between having to be any of those three cats and being able to develop a sense of security.

Frankly, conception doesn't happen with a big red flashing warning light screaming "WHAT ARE YOU THINKING?!?" and admonishments from heaven about what it takes to be really present and there for a child.

Especially only seconds, minutes, hours from the moment of getting started (right, the afterglow).

I think a lot of people end up having to act like those three cats, and sometimes they—we— don't even know which one we are.

The problem is, when the three cats use your garden to scratch in, what they leave behind is not good for the plants

First Things First

There's no adult birds-and-bees lecture about the devotion and love it really takes, the willingness to stand as a Praetorian guard, the shield between that Little Person and the world.

Only that lecture about "don't make babies."

But babies there are. Life BBEY—"bee-bay" which backwards sounds kind of like "bay-bee"—is the time when the most development occurs in our body, our brain, and our systems of learning. It's "Before Birth and Early Years."

Happy factors: strong loving connections to others, emotional coping skills, and sense of worth for just being!

It's not often babies get it all, and it's not about the net worth or dollar value of a family.

BBEY. It's the development of the deeply dug, double tilled garden soil in which is planted for you until you take it over a measure of Happy and a measure of Unhappy.

Even with enough

- Money to take care of the family
- Emotional availability to be present when times are tough (from the Little Person's point of view first and foremost)
- Connection to themselves and others

- Support to have something of themselves left over at the end of the day

parents or caregivers still sometimes fall apart in their ability to be present for their child.

Sometimes the Big People's gardens are too full, too demanding, too overgrown, and there's too much to do—and not enough of the Big People to go around.

Is anyone perfect? Hardly. The balance of event, response, supports, resources, genetic predisposition, development—all these play into the impact of human foibles on a Little Person.

The drama of Unhappy can suck us in...

And in those BBEY years you—as a Little Person—don't have the knowledge, the skills or the authority to take care of yourself. Getting food, shelter and clothing depend on the Big People.

Fact of the matter is that those years are really important when it comes to learning what it means to be human and part of a pack, and you're just unprepared as the dickens to figure out what to do.

So life started out perfect for you, right? You were warm, snuggly, loved, welcome, wanted, supported nurtured, bonded, attached and knew it. Oh life was wonderful, you say. Believe it.

Yes. Wonderful.

And what that means is you have more resilience when the stuff hits the fan, because, dear reader, sometime it will.

Something will happen that just fills up your bucket and pours out over the edges to where you can't contain it all.

Disappointment, rejection, anger, sadness and grief, being overwhelmed to the point of being frozen like a popsicle—it's a pretty sure thing you'll get to check that one off.

It could be a tornado, earthquake, fire or hurricane. Maybe financial devastation. Combat or crime—doesn't make a difference, they all demand their time.

Heck, if nothing else, you'll experience heartbreak a time or three. Every relationship—good or bad—ends in tragedy: death or divorce are no fun.

From the first goldfish you brought home bouncing in its little plastic baggie that bellied up, your beloved pet, to the death of your most beloved, death escorts the ones whose presence brought daily happiness to land not yet ours to inhabit.

Left behind, we pine and grieve and tend the gaping wound left behind.

And should our relationships come to an end through some form of divorce—remember the pain of the loss of friends as an adolescent? The first breakup of a love? That, too, is the land of loss, even when the divorce is absolutely the right, life-saving thing to do.

Unhappy will find you and invite you in, and the gravity it brings with it is strong. It's like Kudzu, the miracle Japanese erosion-controlling vine brought to the US that grows up to 20 inches a day. You don't want to stand still and wait on it.

Happy helps you cope.

The sun still shines, you still have others who care for you, and even when you can acknowledge the benefit of the loss, there is still a vacuum in time, energy, thought, and emotion.

While the sadness, loss, anger, and despair are normal and need voice and existence to dissolve over time, it's also just as important to invite Happy in as well.

Consciously.

Why? Nature abhors a vacuum. As the Unhappy dissolves, something will take its place. You can choose what that is—and I hope you will.

Unhappy plants bloom, fruit, wither, and dry up. You **can** replace them with seeds from Happy. Over time, they'll crowd out Unhappy.

The more Happy you plant and tend and harvest, the more Happy you know and love, the more Happy you can muster and apply, the better you can handle whatever comes your way and in the process grow... more Happy.

Redecorate Unhappy: be the fashion designer of your own life!

The garden that got started for you BBEY is the perfect soil for transformation and change for the rest of your life.

That old Unhappy Hole changes every day, as long as you're plowing, planting the seeds that bring more Happy and tending the plants.

Reupholster that old arm chair down there! Open up the curtains in the Unhappy Hole! Add a few bright flowers and delicious vegetable plants! Pretty soon it will transform—especially if you are persistent.

I still think it's just a dadgum miracle anybody grows up with any degree of Happy. I know that reflects my BBEY stuff, and it was those awful years of triple Rahu on the Rampage. (Or the Devil on a wild bender).

Like I said, I decided to hate Happy (even though I could look like I was Happy) after it seemed so impossible to have or be Happy.

When you ponder on it, the idea that I could make a difference by hating Happy is poignant, funny, and sad.

If you were one of the lucky ones who grew up with a sizable Happy garden, good for you. You can always enlarge it! Model it for the rest of us (and may we keep our eyes open).

How's your Happy? Remember what it feels like?

Are You Happy?

So how's your Happy? Got any? What kind? How much? Does it last long? Can you call it up at will? Is your Happy garden a single plant or a plantation full?

I remember what I think to be the first time I remember recognizing I had fallen into a drunkenly luscious heavenly fruited blend of Happy. I may have had other such epiphanies, and this one was different.

Different enough that I claim it as a hallmark. It was 1997, spring. I was walking down a shaded sidewalk on the Peabody School of Education campus at Vanderbilt University.

Something I never thought I could achieve was about to happen, and in a grand way: I was about to receive a

Masters Degree, a graduate degree, when I barely made it through college (and high school was a nightmare)! Me! On a full scholarship, no less.

What I could never have afforded, if I'd been smart enough to get in, and able to keep it together to finish, and brave enough to apply for had happened. And I'd done it well.

I'd cleared out a substantial space in my big old Unhappy Hole and tried some new plants, and even though some of them didn't make it (I stepped on a couple, a couple got eaten by bugs, and some just didn't sprout), there was a strong and plentiful harvest—undeniably.

I felt this surge of emotion coming up from my feet, like a golden warmth as if the sun were rising way down in my spirit, and all I could do was jump up and down and holler in glee.

It's a good thing not too many people were near by because I think it might have made them think I was on the lunatic train.

Cause of lunacy: a sudden attack of Happy.

Origin of attack: Final elimination of weeds including false stupidus majora, drooping betsimania, and the major belief: "I'm not smart enough, rich enough, acceptable enough to ever get a graduate degree. Let alone from a place like Vanderbilt!"

It was an amazing attack of Happy. It began, for me, a higher level of devotion to continuing what had been planted and was struggling to survive: increases in Happy that longed to fill my garden that could only do so as I was willing to convert the Unhappy over.

I did not die, or experience something awful, or pay a big price, for the Happy. I simply drank in, soaked in it like a brazen lush in a pool full of liquor.

A Happy attack: sweet liquor that sends the soul skyward!

Matching Happy?

Does when you get your Happy up match when most other people do? Do you laugh and act happy when everyone else is crying and sad?

(This is not a good sign, by the way, because unless it's a crowd headed for a brawl or a gang headed to a shooting, you **generally** want to feel what most of people who are not locked up feel in similar circumstances.)

Now there is good reason to vary in some circumstances. A crowd can work up riotous behavior very quickly, heading towards a brawl because everyone wants to be enough like the next person to keep from getting hurt. Avoid that. Turn and walk the other direction.

Or maybe you are hanging with a crowd that is still farming the land of Unhappy. Those seeds will travel—I promise!

If you are a person with some form of disability, and you do well (better than the rest of your PWD community) you are likely to be both the subject of scorn (because they—the PWD—are jealous) and the subject of adoration (the non-PWD community) will be amazed at how well you have done.

My favorite site for a Happy check: www.authentichappiness.org

People With Disabilities (PWD) have a culture too, and part of the management of spoiled identity is fitting in.

A few people, who maybe should do a little treatment time, are Happy when something really bad happens, or get enraged if others express Happy.

We don't count them in this pool, because this pool is about a set of role models who you think are just one or two or maybe thirty steps beyond where you are.

You may be numb, or you may have a little too much hair-trigger (you know, from flat to mad a little too fast). You just want to think about moving a little more into the Happy zone.

Again, how's your Happy? How would you **know** how your Happy is?

Oh, yeah, I can tell you—check out (in the secrecy of your own mind) your thought life:

- How often do you think thoughts that plant something in the Happy Garden (or the Unhappy Hole)?
- Try walking around with a recorder running and grab some of your conversations in the day to day experience
- Listen to them
- Count the no, not, never, couldn't, wouldn't, shouldn't, wouldn't, won't, no, but, if, and if onlys
- Do your thoughts reflect aggression or compassion?
- Is the model of civility they reflect closer to Homer Simpson or the Beaver's parents?
- Are your thoughts focused on what is good, positive, restorative of relationship and respectful of boundaries?
- How much do they reflect cynicism, sarcasm, "attitude," and a need to put someone else down to feel built up?
- How about your emotional life?
- How wide is the breadth of your feeling?

Do a checkup on your:

Thoughts
Language
Feelings

First Things First

- If your emotional life were a garden, how many varieties of plants would it have? How would they look?
- Can you move among those varieties easily and as you choose to?
- Or, do you find yourself either flat or flaring?
- Of the landscape, how many of the feelings are of the pleasant or positive variety?
- The unpleasant or negative? The flat fury in a cold bed of snow type? The "I can't afford to feel" or "I don't know how"?

Would you talk to other people the same way you talk to you?

All you're doing here is exploring and counting—hold off on making any judgment about what this might mean about you because most of the time that is just old Unhappy trying to get you to drop in some fertilizer.

I mean of **course** you feel guilty about things you ought to feel guilty about! And, no, you'd rather clean toilets than be around that old so-and-so!

Feeling bad about the things about which we need to feel bad (so there's some impetus to consider change) is healthy.

It's reconsidering what we're responsible for as Happy gets bigger that's the challenge we all face. I'll ramble about that more later, for now: it's probably more (or less) than you think you're responsible for now.

You doing well in your relationship with you? How often do you beat yourself up in your thoughts?

You know what I mean: you eat something off your diet, and the consequence is not only the change in your body, it's the hours of "I can't believe how stupid I am! I can never stick to a diet. I'm just doomed to be a fat slob. No wonder people don't like me..."

Self-inflicted violence takes many forms—and still it serves a purpose.

What's the level of risky behavior and how's your relationship with it—are you using food, sex, drugs, alcohol or the way you drive to deal with how you feel?

How balanced is work and recreation? That's a big issue.

How well do you listen to yourself? Oh yes, you do need to give yourself praise and advice.

What guidelines do you use to make decisions?

Be honest, now. What are the things you do to exact a price from yourself?

To cause yourself pain? You know them, you know what they are.

Are you a cutter? Burner? Hitter? No? Never would do such a thing?

Do you work sixty hours a week? Burn the midnight oil because the project is the most important thing? Avoid setting boundaries you really prefer? Binge on sweets when you feel badly (or should)?

What's **your** means of expression?

Even today I found a new one: the role of food and self-hate is a different form of violence on my life.

Don't need to binge and purge (which isn't about food anyway), all I need is to travel. I eat bread galore and even the occasional fried (gasp!) food, saying to myself, it's not so bad. Green is usually reserved for décor.

Truthfully? I eat these foods that clog my arteries, substitute for happiness, and increase my portable assets because they make me feel better. I'm lonesome and homesick.

Food becomes my friend, a drug that makes me feel better when I am isolated.

When you can say "this is part of who I am" without all the drama the self-inflicted violence causes, you take away some of its need to be here.

Without harming it or you. And if you have always been kind, loving and compassionate to yourself, great.

Self-compassion is as important (and difficult to develop) as compassion for others. I think about the requirement to love others as I love myself.

If I make myself out to be someone who's fine, filled with love, and loving others while I'm gnawing on myself like a coyote in a trap, how's that going to work?

Love for self grows. It takes tending, and considering. It takes owning the love you have and adding to it, bit by bit.

It's not that love that lets you think too much of yourself (a form of pride) or even asks you to "go above your raising" as they say.

It just asks you to think about what your hatred (part of that big old Unhappy Hole) really means. Preference is one thing, hate is another. And whatever real estate in your head and heart is occupied by hate is a place where love can only visit (and usually run).

Let love come in, visit, dwell in the darkest places.

Let light shine little by little more.

Where darkness was, when light prevails, new life grows.

And in the garden of love, life increases.

Chapter Three: What Getting Happier Gets You

Clearly this whole Getting Happier notion is about stress reduction and management in some ways, and in others it's about doing something about things that hold you back. The benefits are still the same.

A Better Heart.

Nothing personal—this is something you really do want even if you don't know it. Believe me. When you're healthy, you can do a lot of things.

Getting Happier: reduced stress, better life, even without more money!

And when you're young and invincible, all the warnings in the world on a can of DDT are nothing when that truck comes around spraying in the streets.

In the fifties, every child I know was intrigued by the fog and the swirls it would make. Of course that was a long time ago, and now we know that DDT, however effective, had risks.

We also know a lot of other things carry risks. Long term consequences such as five legged frogs and not being able to play outside at all are very annoying to say the least.

We know breathing ANYTHING besides the purest, cleanest air clogs our lungs and ultimately makes it harder for our hearts. We know that all those delicious fried candy bars, French fries, and greasy meat that tasted so good clog us up but good.

We know that smoking and exposure to airborne particles clogs the lungs and increases the risk of heart attacks. Makes it harder to breathe, get oxygen to our brains.

Poor circulation affects more body parts than you think...

Here's a general rundown of why you want the best heart health you can have:

- Poor circulation slows you down, makes you cold, and can cause lots of problems where the blood doesn't flow well (toes, fingers, other things—you know)
- Cholesterol meds can be very expensive and always carry the risk of some sort of side effects you might not enjoy. Better to avoid them
- Strokes can really leave you fried and frustrated. Not much fun to drag, droop or drool from the bad ones
- Heart attacks slow you down; dead heart muscle just doesn't come back
- Hardening of the arteries occurs anyway, and just gets worse a whole lot quicker if you smoke, carry on, and do those risky things you might have come to love.

It's all expensive, and who has the cash for it?

Part of the problem is that according to some studies (like Felliti's ACEs Study—www.acestudy.org), there are nine things that can happen that result in a really big increase in your risks for some kinds of heart disease (and lots of other diseases).

In addition to the usual suspects of abuse and neglect, absence of a parent for any reason prior to age 18, divorce, a parent addicted to alcohol or drugs, growing up with domestic violence or a parent in prison are all part of the famous nine.

If you are visible to others in your world, and if others respond to you in life-giving ways, you are safe

Covers the store front pretty thoroughly when you look at the numbers and, frankly, most of our lives. Every person in every crowd I've been in seems to have one or more of those events from childhood, and, while it may be the crowd I run with, it looks like a public health epidemic to me.

I add another one that I will be pretty clear that the shakier the hookup with your mother ("bonding and attachment") the more invisible you are—and the more vulnerable.

I've maintained for some time that the perfect prey for any predator (Unhappy included) is prey that is invisible. Hard to figure how the invisibility fosters healthy hearts.

What Getting Happier Gets You

As long as I can remember, ever since I had an exotic childhood disease called "St. Vitus Dance" or Sydenham's chorea I have had one or two repetitive dreams.

Because of the St. Vitus' Dance, I was kept in twilight on phenobarbitol for about a month. I haven't had This One Dream in about ten years now,. Yet I can still remember the first time I had it the spring and summer I was sick.

Unhappy begs you to:
- *Go further*
- *Do more*
- *Stay longer than Happy does*

This dream is of me at that age in a red calico dress my mother made with rick-rack across the yoke of a Punjabi dress top with puffed sleeves. My hair is cut with bangs straight across and I have a very somber look on my face. I have that school picture.

I see my chest open up, without blood or anything surgical, and my heart is taken out and replaced with a new one—I remember it even looking like a human heart with all the fibrous silvery tissue, and the arteries coming off the top, the chambers clear. And my little heart was small, and grey, shriveled. It could barely work.

And in this dream, that new heart was so fine. It swelled with pride, and happiness.

Only no one noticed it except me, and so it kept getting replaced. Over. And over. And my new heart never worked for long.

As I got more skilled managing my dreams, I began to refuse to have that dream.

The last time I had it was when my mother was dying, and then I let that dream in.

I saw myself, a little somber-faced child, and I remember smiling at me, and reaching out my adult hand. I stroked that little girl's hair—my hair—in comfort as she slept, relaxing in to her new perfect heart.

I haven't had that dream since.

Unhappy inclines us to risky behavior

Something else about Unhappy. Unhappy inclines us to risky behavior. All that risky behavior—drinking, smoking, partying, driving fast, stressing up, risky sex—stresses your body.

That "fun" might make you feel better (or not at all) for a little while. You may think it's fun, your body knows the difference (sadly, I might say, as one of those people who didn't miss a trick!) about the long-term cost of the short-term fix.

Unhappy almost begs us to go further, do more, and stay longer than we mean to. It takes a toll on our heart.

Laughter, a byproduct of Happy, lowers your blood pressure. As much as we hear about hypertension, good old high blood pressure, anything we can do to reduce it is good.

What Getting Happier Gets You

Especially if it's free. I tell you, laughter sure does light that up that old Unhappy Hole. It's important to have a well-lit Unhappy Hole, I tell you. Believe me.

Once more, it's about your heart—that's the big one. If you can't pump blood strongly enough to reach the outer edges of that old husk you call a body, or if your blood doesn't carry enough oxygen, well, you don't feel good.

It'd be a poor thing to get your Happy up and not be able to enjoy it!

If you paint your lungs with tar and pollutants, you can't take in enough oxygen to feed your blood. If you're a man, having a weak heart from all that stuff can make it hard—well, not hard at all, if you'll pardon the pun.

You'd hate to get your Happy up and not be able to do much with it. All those years you could have done the Happy dance a whole lot bigger! And that takes the healthiest, strongest heart you can muster. No matter what your age is, start your heart on the Happy path—now.

If you happen to be under fifty, even better. If you're under thirty, you have a great chance to get your heart healthy as the dickens. Wherever you are, start now.

If you get Happy, and don't like it, you can always do some damage to your heart health later, but if you damage it now, you may have real trouble getting it back. Trust me.

Improved Health.

All right, we know getting your Happy up helps your heart. It's true.

However, better heart health is not the only health-related benefit of Happy. Here are a few more.

Laughter is a natural painkiller

Natural painkillers.

There are enough research studies now that we know laughter (usually related to happiness, although happiness is not required for laughter) is good for you—it makes your body produce more natural pain killers. And, people who are happier seem to experience lower levels of pain.

It's so vital that there are even laughter clubs in some of the bigger cities in North America and a whole yoga of laughter spreading around the world.

The concept of "holy laughter" has been around for a long time, even though a lot of us forgot how to laugh period unless we were using something to help.

What Getting Happier Gets You

Stronger immune system.

Being happier makes you less likely to get sick: I mean, if you like living and life, your body is probably less likely to attack itself and conversely, probably better able to defend itself.

That old shell you live in is more likely to be thinking—at whatever cellular activity like thought occurs—"living is OK."

We give out more than smoke signals to our body: we tell it what we want from it

There is more and more evidence that stress, unhappiness, and negative feelings (whether you recognize them or not) make it harder to muster the immune system in response to illness.

Longer periods of better health.

Ironically, people who have more Happy in their lives seem to have lower levels of chronic illness.

It only make sense if you think about it—why wouldn't your body gnaw on its own arm so to speak if it got the message that life was awful, people didn't like you, everything was a problem?

I mean, come on. What we know about molecules and those little bitty things that make them indicates they do indeed have some degree of something we might call awareness. They get it.

Longevity.

More Happy means more life, longer life, better life. It doesn't guarantee better sex, more money, satisfaction, contentment, the right partner, or a promotion.

Happy begets Happy—which helps when Unhappy happens

It can bend you towards those, and it can help you get there.

The best prize of all is that Happy makes you want to live longer, and helps you do it—so what happens becomes a continuous, self-seeding and feeding cycle. Just like Unhappy, the plants are self-sowing perennials that multiply feely.

Did you know one of the most common bacteria in dirt helps our immune systems ignore harmless pathogens? That it makes people feel better, like an antidepressant?

All this time we spend trying to manage feeling bluer than blue and one answer might be in the grubbing around we do growing plants.

Try it—search the Internet for "depression garden dirt bacteria" and see what you find.

More Access In Life.

Now it's true that honey draws more flies than vinegar, which, if you want flies is a good thing.

It's also said that you need to dig your well before you get thirsty. Both of these are true. There was a diner not too far—maybe five miles—from the house when I was growing up.

This little joint (The Dome, it was called) also had a motel beside it, marked by the painted metal dome on top of the restaurant, which thrived on lunch orders from furniture workers in the factories that nearly surrounded it.

Happy opens doors..it really does.

It had more flies than you can imagine—the food must have been good, because 10,000 flies couldn't all be wrong! To a fly, the food there was heaven, the honey of fly-dom.

By the same token, those clear zip lock bags filled with water and hung in the diner above the booths kept flies away—they were the vinegar side of this story. For whatever odd little reasons, flies don't like those clear bulging sides and just stay away.

Test it yourself on the actual ingredients! Put a saucer of honey and a saucer of vinegar side by side and **see what each one attracts. Leave** them there for a day or two in the summer time and you'll get a real feel for the situation. Are you vinegar or honey?

Happy opens doors. It makes it easier to get things done, complete tasks, learn new skills, enjoy what happens, make choices in your healthy self-interest.

Of course, people who have big old Unhappy Holes—caverns and canyons of Unhappy—sometimes get lots of access too. And what happens when they do? Can they make a positive difference in the world? For other people?

They might build business empires, set up foundations, and give away money as well as pay salaries. Yet they're still tilling Unhappy for themselves, which is sad.

Healthy Happy helps your relationships

Worse? It's embarrassing to be stuck in Unhappy. When you realize it, the shame is pretty tough.

More Connections.

It's all about networking—in life, there's some kind of invisible web. If you never get on it, or fall off of it, you miss out on a lot of opportunities. It's how people really get work.

Want to up your chance of being employed in tough times? Meet more people? Make friends more easily? Have longer-lasting relationships?

The bigger and more solid your Happy, the longer you have it, the better your connections to yourself and others can be. Remember that chemical oxytocin?

What Getting Happier Gets You

I don't have any clue if this is true or not, but it just makes sense that healthy Happy—a little like being in good love with yourself—ought to increase it.

Bet they'll find someday that it does, and that it makes you healthier in the process.

Better Happy, better connections

I'll tell you this—it's surely easier to be around someone Happy compared to someone whose disposition makes them act like they were raised on dill pickles. And if you consider your relationship to you, Happy can only help. Most of us have more than plenty Unhappy we hang on to.

Stronger Relationship with the Divine. I don't much like to mess with anybody's spiritual relationship, and I'll tell you this much: if you're Jewish, Muslim, or Christian, God tells you that you are God's beloved.

It can't get any better than that even if we don't know what to do with it. Or if we get hung up feeling like we aren't worth what it means to be God's beloved.

Then again, there's enough guilt and shame in the world's religions to pave over every Happy place in the world.

Don't get me wrong—there's guilt we should ought to feel, and guilt we need to pluck out and burn with the thistles. Appropriate guilt helps us know where to draw the boundaries on our behavior.

Now most of us have a lot of trouble with that, even though we might know it in our heads, getting it through to our hearts and into our love for ourselves (without becoming real narcissistic jerks) is another story.

Happy needs appropriate guilt for healthy fences

Each of the Abrahamic traditions (Abraham is the common ancestor for all three) centers on a people uniquely loved by their Creator. Each focuses on the love expressed in a unique way, and, on how people are separated from that love. How people can be reunited with it.

Problem: if you can't take love in, it doesn't do you much good. At its finest, Happy penetrates the spirit, the soul, and helps erode the contempt for the self so that you can take in this love that is there.

That contempt, usually based in how we condemn ourselves, is a weed that can overtake our Happy garden and fill a cavern of Unhappy the size of the Grand Canyon if we don't master it.

If we can move it aside, clear some of that Unhappy to plant the

Happy, so that the love of the Divine can take root, our compassion for ourselves can increase.

Our contentment with who we are picks up. Lonesome old Happy perks up her (or his) ears and trots along. OK, so Happy just went from a plant to a pet.

It doesn't make much difference: it's just that Happy begets Happy, like all of those begats and begots in early scripture where genealogy was critical.

Loving others as you love yourself is better with Happy.

Happy—from just the littlest bit to acres and acres of it or as much as a whole slew of beagle dogs tracking a scent—is a natural reflection of how it seems the Creator wants the Creation to be.

Want a stronger and more positive relationship with the Divine? Add Happy. I don't mean plastic pleasant, I mean Happy.

Getting Happy(er) is a process and it lets the Light (whatever name the Light has in your world) in, which helps it grow. We just have to figure out how to take it in.

The rest of those requirements specific to each tradition are matter you may want to talk to your rabbi, imam, or minister about—and if they really get in your way, find a pastoral counselor in your tradition.

Less Stress.

You'd have to be pretty dense not to get this one. Clearly, if you get all of the other benefits, it's because this has also happened.

You've either reduced the stress to a manageable level or figured out how to handle it better.

Kind of like figuring out how to take a less than desirable garden spot and making it into your own little paradise.

Less stress doesn't guarantee more Happy, but more Happy guarantees less stress

You know, make some raised beds so your back feels better, some permanent rows so you are tilling only the soil you'll plant, crop rotation to help keep the soil healthy—all this from a clay-based yard.

It's nice to say "more Happy means less stress" and it's true, and less stress consists of those positive benefits listed.

Of all the gardens we might sow,

Happiness is sure to grow.

Our choice to happy be

Changes everything we do see.

Chapter Four: Why It's All About You...

You ARE the Most Important Person.

Listen, when you're out in the street with a naked (maybe that's "nekkid..") tukus (behind) flapping in the wind, the chances are exceptionally strong that no one is going to come along and cover it. Unless of course the modesty police just happen to be hanging around.

No matter how much of a martyr ("I only did it for you") type you are, when the chips are down you really only count on yourself (and whatever relationship you have with the Divine).

You can go through a lot people getting from Unhappy to Happy

You can count on others to some extent in the process, and the chances are high that if the Unhappy gets big and ugly enough, almost all of them fall by the wayside. Even the most loyal have limits.

Some recycle around, a few are gone for good.

I can honestly say that the map to get from the big old Unhappy Hole to Happy is a map that includes villages and towns that generally get devastated by the process as you meander, stomp, stroll and storm along the way.

Why It's All About You...

You can burn through a lot of acquaintances, friends, and family getting from one place to the other on the road from the Abyss of an Unhappy Hole to the Heartland of Happy.

So part of why it's all about you is that you have to become the best you possible—the expert coach, the cheerleader, the counselor and mentor to yourself.

Once you have a glimpse of Happy, the taste of its nectar-- You want it.

Getting Happy to grow like a weed, make that an ever-blossoming vine, is to learn how to be your own internal support system.

The truth still remains: it's all about you. The way you learn to think about yourself, feel towards yourself (which drives how you deal with others), and act—all your patterns—focus on you. Plain and simple.

Everything Revolves Around You.

Everything. Yes. The whole world revolves around you. It **is** all about what you want, need, deserve, require to let Happy run rampant like a morning glory on a fence.

You're the only one, once you get to a certain age, who can decide what you want in that garden that makes up your life. It may be one of the few choices over which you have full control.

You're the only one who can identify the plants and why they're there, which ones are weeds right now and which ones bear fruit that you like.

Testing the soil for balance and fertility? Yep. You're the only one who can do that, too. And you're the only one who can learn how to plant and tend and harvest the Happy in your life.

Little people need age-appropriate choices (check out child development for more information)

Standing in the garden eating fresh, warm, sweet tomatoes that I just picked, and munching on tiny baby okra, waiting for that first cured sweet potato in the fall?

That's Happy. It brings me a lot more happiness than the thistles and briars I used to chew. Lots more.

You're the Only One Who Can Change You.

What that means is that as the center of your little universe, you're in charge or you. Not anyone else or their actions, only yours.

Now it is very true that you can only live what you learn. And this means that whatever patterns you learned as a child you practice growing up.

Why It's All About You...

Fact is, almost everyone is stuck in their own patterns, the things they learned, the ways of doing and being to survive, make do and thrive.

Little People should really only make choices they can handle developmentally. They need to make age-appropriate choices.

Little People make Little People choices, like what food they want (although the Big People help them get balanced diets and healthy foods); as they grow up, what clothes to wear (and Big People are responsible for matching these to weather, norms, and culture); the kinds of movies and books and toys they want (with Big People censorship in place).

We live what we learn—and as we mature, we can change that

You follow the layout, right? The bigger Little People get, the more Big People decisions they make—with the Big People's help. Over time, they become responsible for all their choices.

They become Big People.

Big People are responsible for themselves. Only there's a catch. You learned how Big People act from the Big People you grew up around.

Whatever they modeled, you learned. Chances are you learned their patterns even if they show up a little differently in your life. The ones that you like, the ones you don't like. Truthfully?

You're the only one who can change you. That means you're the only one who can take action in your own life. I mean—the garden that got planted for you as a child is something you can stick with or change.

Whatever got planted then is not what you are required to keep planted now: changing crops takes time, and oh boy howdy effort. Your effort.

Then again, it's your garden and your life—yours—and you are the only one who can do anything different.

You are the only one living in your body, thinking in your head, acting with your hands, feeling your feelings and doing what you do.

Unless the Cosmic Gardener performs an instant-change miracle, the choices that you make over time to create change are all yours to make. That's why it is all about you.

OK. I'm through with that rant.

You
are the only one who matters.

If you become genuinely happy,
happy for the sake of happy,

imagine
how much more love you will have to share.

Chapter Five: Do Your Emotions Have You on the End of Their Leash?

Getting from the Short to the Long End of the Leash.

Of all the things people need getting from the BBEY to some form of adulthood, there are a couple that just top the tree. Now some folks would say all three of these have to be present, and of course they need to be present at some optimum level. The truth of it is that you deal with what you get.

Remember those tourist gizmos: invisible dogs on leashes? It's like that. (You can still buy them!)

First of all, you get from one end of the leash to another by being able to be present. You can weed a lettuce bed if you know it's there, and you know where the edges are (of course, it helps if you can recognize a lettuce leaf!).

Second, you have to believe you matter, or have some sense over time of worth. Notice that I didn't describe what matter means—contempt and hate are as strong as compassion and love.

If your goal is to show Happy a thing or two and you're dedicated to it, you have an enduring sense of worth. If your goal is show Unhappy a thing or two, and you're dedicated to it, that too is a sense of worth. You can change your sense of worth.

Do Your Emotions Have You On the End of Their Leash?

Finally, the better you are making and maintaining healthy connections with other people the easier it is to move from one end of the leash to the other end of it!

Again, I didn't say **ideal**, and healthy is a moving target. Just like keeping the soil just right in any garden—Happy, Unhappy or otherwise—takes knowing what it needs and feeding it the right nutrition. So does making healthy relationships of different sorts.

Emotions run amok: invisible owner in the dog's harness!

What does the short end of the leash look like? Think about these indicators that point towards the short end of the leash.

- Do your emotions ride a roller coaster you didn't get a ticket for?
- Is everything personal?
- Do your eyes have faucets with someone else turning the handles?
- Are your feelings plastered all over your sleeves?
- Do people tell you not to take everything so personally?
- Do you seem to emit the gradual odor of skunk, resulting in frequent loss of friends?
- Is everything always (or most often) your fault (according to you, and maybe everyone else)?

Do Your Emotions Have You On the End of Their Leash?

- Do you cry at all the sad songs, you know, at the music they play when those pretty dog food commercials come on TV?
- Is your idea of dealing with a breakup to drink a six-pack?
- Do you feel like you have very little control over what you feel?

You get the drift: when it feels like your emotions have you on the wrong end of the leash, it's not much fun. You can leave a pretty wide swath of destruction behind you.

The stronger your Happy, the better you can manage tough times

Now if it's all you know, don't you reckon this is your own personal version of "normal"? I'm pretty certain it is.

The normal I learned—Mama, bless her heart and in retrospect, was probably really depressed. Who knows! It may have started with post-partum and been jumped on by grief given her life from 1954 or so on. Compounded to clinical darkness galore.

I know this: the Mama ***I*** grew up with in the privacy of our home was sometimes darkly forlorn, lonesome, sad, and in pain underneath her facial expression. But she "had game," and made sure she was as there as she could be for us.

The Mama that I knew from the mid-seventies was someone very different from the Mama I remember as a child. Her transformation was profound and wonderful. And it took work on her part.

I'm going to say again: it's always good to jack up Happy. That means you can get around to the end of the leash and get behind your emotions instead of being in front of them.

When you're on the front end of the leash, your emotions pretty much walk (or run) you wherever they want to go without a lot of concern for the longer term consequences.

You can choose—with practice, and most of the time, how you feel.

That's power.

Emotions want to be felt now-- **n-o-w** now, without any interference. While sometimes this is the perfect, right thing other times it just goes in the other direction of where you want to be.

And clean up takes a lot longer than an initial redirect— which is why it is good to get on the back end of the leash!

Just like training an annoying little yipper, it takes a plan, consistency, and rewarding the behavior you want (while ignoring what you don't want). More about that later.

And believe me, there's always change, so don't expect to stand still on the back end of that leash! There's usually a lot of dancing around while you're moving "normal" to a new definition.

Even when you get there, the world around you changes. This dance of "which end of the leash" is a lifelong one.

You just get better and better at it, and better at choosing which end you want to be on (and getting there).

Choosing Your Feelings

Power for the Self.

I "choked" delivering a ten minute segment of a training audition. I missed my cue. I felt the burning hot flames of embarrassment and heard the shame machine roar to life.

I could feel myself teetering on the handles of a big tiller about to buck me into rocky soil, tines glinting at the coming victory of shame and despair.

OMG as they text—oh my G-D—as I felt myself sinking, plummeting into the dark void of forever marked by one moment in time.

I was lucky. I've practiced getting off the horns of that particular dilemma, or backing down off the handles of the bucking tiller, and I've practiced enough that I had some reserve—for a time just like this one.

I turned and asked the expert next to me to navigate to the right place in the application.

Do Your Emotions Have You On the End of Their Leash?

Even though I could feel the burning flame of shame creeping up and threw off my sweater to keep from exploding, I was able to keep my thoughts balancing my emotions (I'm not always so lucky).

Talking to myself I was saying, "keep going, keep going, the best performers recover and keep going—this feels much worse than it actually is."

I finished thanked them, walked to my seat, and decided the praise people were giving me was just consolation and was terrified I had cost my client their contract.

I was sure of it.

When the client representative stood up and said we all did great I was still convinced she was lying through her teeth and the shoe would fall privately.

I was still convinced of how badly I had done, and work as I might, no matter how much I said that it could feel awful and in fact be fine, I was having trouble walking that plank over the muddy ravine.

Sometimes it is SO hard to get from Unhappy to Happy! It is as if muck-monsters reach up from the mud and try to drag us down into darkness. And I've made up my mind to do my part and slog forward.

When I apologized to her for doing so poorly, she looked at me like I was nuts. She told me I was one of the best (no offense to everyone else, but it sure surprised me!).

I decided I was the one who had been lying—didn't mean to, of course, but my emotions had me on the short end of the leash.

And, if I'd been tilling, I'd have done double backflips and been soundly thrashed by the tiller.

My hands would have been "duck-taped" to the handles on the tiller, though, and I'd have gotten to the end of the row or the yonder side of the garden come hell or high water.

As you master yourself, you master the universe

Self-mastery is the ultimate Happy. May not make you rich or attract the "perfect" mate. Won't always feel good right in the moment.

The feelings and the facts may not match for a while, just as they didn't for me.

None the less, by being able to tolerate the feelings and recognize they didn't have to match the facts, when I heard enough evidence that my feelings were out of alignment with the facts, I could relax and let go of them. I could make room for some others that were part of Happy.

Do Your Emotions Have You On the End of Their Leash?

Mastery of (not over) self is the perfect soil for Happy to sprout in. Every single one of us can enrich that soil, keep making it more and more attractive to Happy.

If we focus on Unhappy, spouting and sowing it wherever we are, thinking, feeling and speaking it, it just gets bigger and bigger.

Sometimes Unhappy is so important we reframe Happy to Unhappy because it's more familiar. The same effort can be refocused to see if Happy is to be found.

Energy doesn't care how it is directed

Happy has as many varieties and degrees as Unhappy! The same energy can be used in any direction you choose, even if it takes you a while to learn how.

Planting the seeds of the power and learning to use that power with yourself means identifying and practicing choices over and over—even when (not if) they feel weird. Seeds usually do when they're popping out of their jackets.

Happy's made of lots of choices: choices to consider, to be open to, to suspend, to deflect, adopt, rehearse, practice, do, repeat, and then to repeat lots more.

Do Your Emotions Have You On the End of Their Leash?

Thing is, the more you identify and build up that library of feelings and how to turn the volume up and down, the more mastery you have of, with, and over yourself.

Just a heads-up. The power you have? If you use it to be abusive toward yourself, you might want to read this book again.

The point is rather than punishing yourself for how you experience the world, use those feelings as alarms. Look at what sets them off.

See how they can inform you—help them assume a more natural and balanced place in your life.

World class pumpkins win ribbons after lots of choices that add up

New Eyes for the World.

Power for the self—and of you with you (yes—read it again)—relies on being able to frame, and reframe just about every situation under a variety of circumstances—and be aware of when and how you do it.

How do you do that?! How does that single pumpkin seed turn into the 550 pound state fair winner, too? Somebody's making choices and seeing them through, in either case.

Peter who manages that Pumpkin Patch—he chose to plant the seed. He chose not to thin that particular plant. He chose to water and fertilize it. He chose to protect it from things that could harm it.

He chose when to do everything he did relative to that pumpkin in his patch. He chose to move it to a strong supported platform for growth so he could just forklift it on a pallet out of the patch if it turned out good.

Growing Happy is like growing any world class piece of produce—only it lasts longer

Above all, Peter was willing to consider that any of this could happen, that it might be possible to grow a really big pumpkin in his patch of generally ordinary sized pumpkins.

And when he considered that and said "yes, it might be possible to do that" he was planning his next patch.

At the same time he sort of wondered where the best spot in the patch would be for such a plant, so that it would get the best water and light.

And when he planted his pumpkin patch, he did as he generally would, except he heard himself thinking a time or two, "I wonder if I could grow a state fair winner?"

So when this one particular plant showed itself to be stronger and faster growing than the best, and it was clear Peter had plenty of vines, he culled some of the vines around this one. This too was a choice and based on eyes that now saw a different possibility.

Recognizing he had more than the average fall season orange globe developing, Peter made another set of choices—you have to look at harvest differently if you think you have a huge pumpkin in the making. The size, weight, and fragility issues—oh they are something when a pumpkin gets that big!

Optimal choice means defining what optimal means to you

After all, it's a big old hollow thing and you know the walls aren't even and even moving it could make it crack into pieces.

How much water does it need before it begins to go bad? What nutrients should you feed it? How often? What's Mother Nature going to do? How will you get it out of the field?

So Peter, once again thinking wildly about the state fair and all its glory, decided to risk it all on one pumpkin, which he positioned on a palled so he could lift it with a fork truck later on.

All the way to the grandstand to receive the blue ribbon, Peter who runs the Pumpkin Patch had to be willing to see something in addition to his Halloween Jack o'Lantern stand on the corner of Ash and Main in Anytown.

Do Your Emotions Have You On the End of Their Leash?

The Optimal Choice.

What on earth makes a choice optimal? That sounds awfully hi-falutin' (uppity and big-headed). Optimal is about getting the most of what you want from a situation—without hurting the other person.

It's the ideal "win-win"—kind of like when dandelions get a second life in the garden because they pass as a fancy green to steam and lay under a pecan-crusted filet of rainbow trout. Well, they're good other ways, too, that's just the recipe I thought of as I write this.

Defining "optimal" means comparing choices to consequences

Think about old Peter who runs the Pumpkin Patch. He could have said, "It's just a dadgum old pumpkin patch."

He could have said "So what's another big pumpkin. We just sell 'em all" or "I'm pulling this one up because it's growing too much bigger than the others."

He could have said all kinds of things. What he chose to say and do got him to the platform at the state fair, picking up a ribbon and a check. It also helped him become the positive envy of his farmer friends.

I don't know how he knew. Learning what it takes to trigger you to think in a different way, or to even identify different ways you might think about something, is a process that seems both intuitive and learned at the same time.

Most people know a box has four sides and a top and bottom. And there is a different view from every side, yes. Do they think about it in sides or as a whole?

Where are they "standing" in the picture when they see the box? Inside or out? Corner or side? How many ways can you think of to think about a box?

How many ways can you help yourself think differently about a situation?

Plants know how to grow. They don't care one whit where, if they have fertile soil, light, and water. If there's enough sun, the corn doesn't care if it grows here or there or three rows over.

To make "the optimal choice" means you've identified at least two choices, one which is new to you.

Every year I look at the tomato plants, all kinds of varieties, and while I stick with my favorite ones, I branch out, trying to find a tomato that maybe takes fewer days to maturity, or takes a little less rain. Maybe a lot.

The point is, how do I know there is an optimal choice? Well, I look around. What do other people do when they're in the same kind of situation I'm in?

I wonder, literally, how they act—what they think, and feel? When I wonder that, suddenly lo and behold, I become aware of the possibilities and can think about them.

Because I can think about multiple options, and test them against what I say I want, I can identify the best match. That means I need to figure out what makes one choice more preferable than another.

Of course that means being willing to think. Are you?

Thinkers pay a price.

First of all, it's easy to over-analyze a situation, although as little as most of us demonstrate critical thinking, I suspect that's not as much of a problem as it could be. On the other, it makes people who (to others) over-analyze stand out like sore thumbs.

Second, it makes you look like an egghead. As someone whose childhood nicknames included "Einstein," I can tell you that's hard to deal with as a child. The assumption is that eggheads have no heart.

Finally, when people believe you think "too much" they may believe you feel "too little."

The assumption of an imbalance can truly make an a-double s out of all involved.

It also isolates and alienates the person accused of being too much of a thinker, and the person who makes the accusation.

It also risks putting both people on the collar end of leash because neither usually feels good about the decision to part ways.

The pleasure of denial is not knowing, the pleasure of knowing is the pain of the absence of denial.

Chapter Six: When Being Happy is Crazy in Drag (OK, It's Really Not All About You!)

We All Know Denial is More Than a River.

There are people who would swear they're Happy—and in their world, they are. The problem is that their world is just that: only theirs!

You know the type; you might have been there somewhere along the way. Makes as if everything in their little garden of life is good, and their language just fairly shrieks a major weed alert.

People in denial genuinely don't know that they don't know

They'd be smiling and laughing if a rattlesnake was latched on them, saying everything will be fine because of their belief that it will be, or using phrases and words that uncover the contempt, judgment, and mistrust they feel.

It might always be the other person, or that everyone is out to get them, or they live in a world of mistrust—whatever the nature of the big old Unhappy Hole they're in, they are clueless that it's not Happy Heaven.

If you're there, you won't know it. That's the nature of denial. And no telling will help you believe it. You'll be there until it's time for you to get somewhere else, on a timetable that no one else can control

If you're there, a lot of other people might know it. And they can for sure tell, and wonder what to do about it. They can't tell you: you won't listen. They can't prove it: you won't see. They are affected by it, and generally powerless over your denial.

Denial protects us from knowing dangerous things

No matter what people told me, thinking I might be intelligent was on everybody's menu but mine.

Intelligent people didn't grow up and amount to as little as I did. These intelligent people made better grades, had higher test scores, and better jobs than I did. They were in what appeared to be "good" relationships. Therefore I was not intelligent.

I could find every excuse in the world to hold my foot down on my own neck like I was pinning down a copperhead in the garden. I didn't dare let up.

When I finally decided I was intelligent, I saw how foolish I'd been by insisting on how stupid I was. Thankfully, I was able to laugh at myself and then pat myself on the back instead of spiraling into shame when my denial crumbled.

When Being Happy is Crazy in Drag
(OK, It's Really Not All About You!)

We all cling to our denial. It serves an important protective role in our lives, keeping us from knowing things we can't afford to know. In my gardening, I generally choose to stay in denial (which means it's not really denial) about winter.

I plant cool crops too late in the season, blithely ignoring the fact of frost, sleet, snow, and icy cold winds **knowing** I'll have some form of lettuce or greens (in addition to turnip greens)and spring onions in December, and perhaps still fresh dill, parsley and coriander in January. My neighbors knowingly look at me like I'm nuts.

Maslow's hierarchy of learning:

- *Unconscious incompetency*
- *Conscious incompetence*
- *Conscious competence*
- *Unconscious competence*

No contest there (maybe). Two years in a row I've had some fresh produce on my table January 1. I don't even consider the weather an issue. I plant because seeds grow into plants. The rest just happens.

Now everyone around me knows it's not that simple and I really do too (which means—it's not really denial, if it's denial you don't know that you don't know).

I like to think of a guy named "Maslow" and his hierarchy of learning. Maslow says the first stage in learning is "unconscious incompetence"—you don't know that you don't know.

When Being Happy is Crazy in Drag (OK, It's Really Not All About You!)

To me, this is a lot like denial. My gardening is a lot like that when it comes to some plants: I just shrug. Or, perhaps it's like a bed I once planted where I was certain of the seed: only I was certain in my error: the seeds were not in fact what I thought they were!

The next level on Maslow's hierarchy is where I am with regard to winter planting: conscious incompetence. I **know** that I don't <u>know</u> about a lot of plants and how to grow them.

We are more than what we do—so much more!

This is similar to when I got fed up with my Unhappy Hole and decided to renovate—I had to learn all the skills so I could do the work. It's work you can't hire out, though you can hire a coach or therapist.

That renovation was, and is, more expensive than moving. Every time I try that, I find I've dragged Unhappy with me. It's really an internal landscaping issue instead of an external one!

When Your Face is About to Crack From that Old Fake Smile.

The other crazy in costume is the person who is crying, angry, or in despair on the inside and acts like everything is fine—and knows it.

When Being Happy is Crazy in Drag (OK, It's Really Not All About You!)

There is not much to say except that if you are this person (and I was for some time), take time and find someone (besides your friends) where it is appropriate for you to peel back that mask.

Get inside of it. It'll take time, and you can wear less and less of it as you jack up your Happy.

The only mask I want to wear is made of mint and mashed cucumber.

No matter how broad or expansive you consider your Happy or your Unhappy, others may see you differently than you see yourself.

Remember: a weed is only a weed when it's where you want another plant to be.

It's Harder to Be Helpful If You're Not Happy

Is happiness a prerequisite to doing good and being helpful?

Or is doing good and being helpful a prerequisite to being happy? This one could go either way.

Sometimes it's parents, or maybe culture, that inclines us to "do good" no matter how we feel. You know: "you don't have to like it, you just have to do it—and to the best of your ability."

We connect our worthiness to our actions, we decide we're good or bad based on what we do to, for, or with others. We decide who we are through whatever is reinforced. That's the identity we take on.

Big People help Little People learn what it means to be helpful, and how Happy works

Oh yes. You know, they (whoever "they" are) say that if you call someone a duck three times, they'll start looking for feathers on their tail. Now imagine you're a Little Person.

Your Big People call you names. They expect you to **(a)** do everything they tell you to, or perhaps **(b)** to do whatever you want to. The best of all possible choices is that they tell you are wonderful, welcome and wanted. That you are OK just as you are.

They compliment you when you do good things. When you do things that cause harm, they allow you to experience the natural consequences without throwing you to the wolves. In these areas, they do the best they can.

They praise you for doing the things Little People like you should do. They recognize your activities as a Big Person instead of joining you from a Little Person perspective.

Their relationships to you are marked by being present, enthusiasm, and language that describes without judgment. By praise, and recognition.

They play with you as Big People playing with a Little Person instead of sliding back into Little Person. (After all, who ever taught them how to do that? We all love to play, right?)

Strong and menacing tones of voice are reserved for moments when significant danger is present, and are used as warnings.

On the other hand, you might have ended up with messages that put you in the car with the cousin most likely to be able to reach you—in the Big People's eyes.

Bless that cousin's heart, they were told to try to straighten you out and steer you away from drugs and sex which you were undoubtedly engaging in!

You might have appeared to be running wild when you could have been pristine and perfect in someone else's eyes.

What if you took in—no matter what the Big People said or did—that something about you is wrong, or uncomfortable to be around? Much of your time from then on will be spent working to make sure that this is the way your world goes.

I so know this routine. So I knew—beyond the shadow of a doubt—that I am not smart enough to get a graduate degree.

If I continued to insult my friends who lived Happy, I might lose them—I had to apply to graduate school to prove them wrong

I cite my evidence: it took me seven years to get a BA: my grade point average was really low, like, somewhere around a 2.10 out of a 4.0.

On the required exam, the GRE (Graduate Record Exam) I never got past the 20th (or maybe lower) percentile on math, eve though I was in the 90th or so in language. I was just not smart enough.

Yet there were so many who said I should go! Then I added being crazy—crazy people shouldn't get graduate degrees. I did everything I could to point out the message I adopted about myself: "You'll never amount to anything." As long as I could get everyone else to believe it with me, I could be comfortable.

Well, I couldn't get them to believe. And one morning I woke up in a cold sweat. If I didn't at least apply, I was insulting the people who acted like they liked me and who I hadn't been able to drive away.

If I applied and didn't get in, they'd get it that I couldn't do the work and... I'd save face and keep getting to be too stupid for graduate school.

The long and short of it is that I get in, and got a full assistantship and except for a few rocky months, made it through with flying colors. I am still amazed at how terrified I was of being intelligent! And I am still sometimes terrified, as if it is one more ruse to keep me separate from feeling like I have a place on this planet.

Expand your care for yourself to be able to expand your care for others

So: feeling like that about myself, how could I be helpful? Most of the time it was duty, trying to make others like me, and feeling like I owed it to the world to do good things (this one may still be true).

Seldom was it out of a happy heart full of the desire to do good for the sake of doing good! I was helpful, and it helped me feel needed.

Needed and **happy** are two different things altogether.

A Cheerful Heart Warms Others' Souls.

It is so true. If you're around people who pull energy from you, you feel like someone pulled the plug on the bathtub of life when you're around them.

They leave you with a chill in your soul and a sense of being sucked empty, turned into a hollow shell, or so tired all you can do is fall in bed. Chances are they're not very cheery, or maybe you sense the cheer isn't real—whatever the cause, you feel drained.

Choose whose Happy you hang around with: match Happy and limit Unhappy in your life

And when you're around those folks who practice re-circulating cheerfulness through the fountain of their heart, they somehow warm your soul. You feel filled up, a little lighter, perhaps a little more alive when you leave them.

You know the ones: somehow they've stepped aside from stress and Unhappy and are tending Happy for a while. They've realized that Unhappy is always ready to dump a load in the Unhappy Hole. They've figured out how to add to Happy, or, they've decided to build up Happy—just because.

How do I know this? Well, I bought a house a while back. It's in an older neighborhood with some of the original folks from the 50s living in the homes of their young dreams.

Their warmth and cheer are genuine, I hope for as long as we are all here, and even if only for a while—relationships, like an old established grape vine, get trimmed back sharply under some circumstances.

Mine waxes and wanes too, depending on the demands of life and how well I'm managing my internal landscape.

Mind you, I'm not talking about the phony cheerfulness that makes us all existentially nauseous or the cheerfulness that pops up every time someone expresses any form of discouragement.

I found dirt as the metaphor for my Unhappy and Happy... what's yours?

It's important to sit with those feelings of discouragement, too, and if you can, avoid visiting them on others.

I used to garden thinking about how good those tomatoes would taste and what that first frost-touched sweet potato would taste like.

I spent all my time digging in the dirt and growing things to either keep remembering the people I loved, or to be able to chop their heads off of the sorry (fill in the blank) over and over.

I started on the chopping side of the equation. All the hate and anger and self-pity and contempt that got poured into that soil. My goodness.

I hope someone has come along who loves that soil in a different way.

My Unhappy poured out into the dirt, was taken in by it, and it is another dadgum miracle the soil didn't just refuse to grow a single thing. The weeds did well, and I coaxed a tomato or two out of it.

In general, it mostly caused my neighbors to marvel at how I could travel so much and make a garden. Over the years, in the two pieces of soil that absorbed all that Unhappy in gardening, and with a lot of other tools and skills, I changed my relationship to gardening.

Unconscious incompetence: we ***don't*** *know that we don't know*

It wasn't just what the dirt, and the worms, and the bacteria, and the plants could do for me, it was also that I came to love the soil. I mean really love it.

I became a servant and I hope leader to the dirt that gives me life, feeds me, helps restore my soul, and brings me such happiness and contentment. I love the soil. I am still learning how to plant and cultivate different kinds of Happy and—I so love the relationship with the soil.

I still don't care for the cabbage worms, or the grasshoppers I war with. And I don't really want a hen to help with that, although the idea is romantic.

I just want to keep loving the dirt and loving how it grows things, loving the cycle of life in the flowers, herbs, vegetables and fruits my garden supports on my behalf. Yes, by golly, I am blessed. My heart often feels cheerful (to me).

I delight in bringing joy to others by being helpful. My boundaries make being helpful and keeping my Happy hiked up easier.

I am blessed. If you ask me how I am, I hope I remember to say it. If I forget, ask me—please: "Are you blessed?"

*Conscious incompetence: we **know** that we don't know.*

If you want an interesting experience, listen to what people say when you ask them how they're doing. "Not too bad," which can be pretty believable most of the time (things can always get worse!); "Fine, thank you," which is the polite don't-dig-any-further answer; and "I'm blessed."

Who's got the cheerful heart among these respondents? Who of all three would you ask for help? Want to spend time with?

"I'm blessed" is the answer of someone who knows what it feels like to be oppressed from without or within or who has learned to see the good in their life.

Someone who now instead of loving that big old Unhappy Hole with its broke down TV and dollar ninety-nine cooler loves Happy. Sows Happy, feeds Happy, you know the drill... Happy.

You can be helpful if you're in misery, it's just a lot more fun when your Happy is up.

Contentment and Happiness: Learned.

Those early years teach us the level of contentment and happiness it's OK for us to have. They help us learn our "normal and how we should "be" in it. When our eyes see more and we see that we can change "normal," the way we express it may not match anymore.

That is as it should be—in the garden, we change and adjust how it lays, how the rows are laid out, sometimes even the row jogs to accommodate a rock or lump.

As things come up, we thin, adjust, feed, water, catering to the needs of each type of plant. If we have been "unconsciously incompetent" about a plant and learn more, we change how we deal with it, and with the requirements it places on the soil.

Of course, contentment starts within, and spreads from internal to external, among friends and even out into communities. The nature of happiness is that it is contagious—Happy spreads just as Unhappy does.

Even plants "talk" and "listen" to one another (search on the term "do plants communicate with one another" and "plants talk to each other"—some of the responses are science based).

What if everything really is somehow connected with everything else? What if what I feel is somehow picked up by not only someone but also something else?

Do I have an obligation to practice Happy? To practice contentment? I can only say this: if what we have in today's world is partially a result of what everyone has been feeling, we are in a heap of trouble.

Practicing Happy may be our greatest contribution to our world

Recessions, depressions, regional conflicts and wars, random attacks of violence and all that other stuff? What kind of feelings contribute to that?

Practicing learned contentment and happiness may not cause any of these to ease up on an apparent worldwide basis. They will surely make you feel better and more able to deal with difficult times.

They may rub off, emanate, radiate or somehow influence your friends and neighbors. That's pretty good. That's juicy.

I could almost feel a little burst of joy at that, because if I can make a positive difference in a realistic way, I think that's a plus.

Happiness serves others

It brings light and life

Like rain it nourishes

Like sun it feeds

Like love it nurtures

Chapter Seven: Extreme Happiness: Joy is Juicy!

A Chronic Condition or an Intermittent Moment?

Now, some people think we should go for joy all the time. I think this is based on the old saying "Shoot for the moon; even if you miss, you'll land among the stars."

The notion of living in ecstasy on an ongoing basis: unrealistic and distracting

It's popular these days to teach that a person can have joy all the time and just live in bliss. Think about the teachings about "the Law of Attraction"—they say you create your own reality, and attract what you think about and teach that if we don't have joy it's because we don't want it, and that if we don't have it, that we didn't contract for it before we got born.

That's pretty scary. This is another example of black and white thinking, the all or nothing way of thinking that makes gardeners strew a whole packet of seeds (or none at all) when they need only a few to get a luxurious harvest.

The problem with considering joy is that if you think it's "all or nothing" then everything in between has very little value.

The truth is that all the shades in between are important, and when you look at those shades, life is lots richer. Lots juicier.

Extreme Happiness:
Joy Is Juicy!

Joy as a continuous state of being is something every mystic and holy person longs for. Those folks tend to be well outside the usual 80% of us, and as a rule, we **hope** to experience moments of joy, or extreme happiness.

Believing in joy should be a chronic condition, even though our **experience** of it may be intermittent. The more we tend the plantings of contentment and Happy that we have, the higher our likelihood of a little Joy now and then.

Believing in happiness should be chronic condition

The challenge is that looking for chronic joy can keep you from experiencing the Happy that is right in front of you. If you are always on the hunt, you may never see the quarry.

The other challenge with joy as something we can control our way into having is that it makes the process very self-centered.

If you control your reality well enough to have what you want or take 100% responsibility for not having what you want, you're bouncing off the walls without any recognition whatsoever of the rest of the world.

This is a peculiar kind of narcissism. Unfortunately, I've just never been able to see myself operating outside of a system, or outside of a relationship with everything around me.

It is in so many ways a careless teaching—it's as if I said to my garden, I don't care that it is winter and 20 degrees Fahrenheit; you will grow lettuce because I want it. And you will grow it abundantly.

Or, perhaps I say: the troubles in my early years were all my parents' fault, or all the fault of Rahu, or all my own choices in play—as if somehow I am 100% aware of and responsible for everything—yes, everything—that happens.

Aim high—and keep aiming, content in each step of achievement as well

Truthfully now: do **you** control everything that happens? I surely know I don't! That grasshopper that chewed the top off of my beautiful bean plants—oh, if you only knew how often I imagined those plants as beautiful, and how seldom I worried about insects!

And old Miss Possum with her draggy down belly? I never imagined or focused on her walking the top of my chain link fence to get the grapes!

Nor did I see or think or want other people to take some of the actions they took. If I controlled everything, we'd all have food, shelter, clothing, and love galore without poverty, neglect and war!

Extreme Happiness:
Joy Is Juicy!

None of us can eat the whole worm when things happen—and we can't expect the other person to either. Seldom is anyone 100% in charge of everything (everything) that happens.

Certainly there are times when the other person owns **much** more than 50% (like the fellow that ran the stop light, accelerating as he went). Defensive driving teaches me to look both ways before I start out, and to wait just a second before gunning it when the light turns green.

On the bathtub curve, the real power is in small controlled swings that control the variation

All I'm saying is this: sit down, take off any blinders you have on and do a three-way sort on your life and who "owns" the choices in it. Anywhere there is another person involved, consider their power too.

In the best relationship, each person manages the 100% that makes up their contribution to it—which varies from day to day.

Aim for Joy and Delight in Contentment.

Yeah, I know—what's the difference between this and that shoot for the moon saying? Not much except you can probably get to contentment easier than the stars, and joy's a lot closer than the moon!

Joy's a lot more sensible as a target—just like Peter in the Pumpkin Patch needed lots of pumpkins that the average people would buy, he knew he had a chance. He knew that two of every ten pumpkins would be "different" one would be a runt, and the other bigger, maybe.

If he grew 100 pumpkins, 20 would be off size, either under or over. Of the 20 he knew two—TWO—would be exceptional. This year, one was the 550 pound lunker state fair winner. The other was smaller and badly misshapen.

Planning and tending Happy carefully produces greater yields

Peter knew, likewise, he couldn't plant only two seeds and except anything exceptional. Planting only two would give his pumpkin patch the Bell Curve syndrome, where 50% of his pumpkins would be above average.

Planting more pumpkins of the best quality seed in the best soil he could create with the right amount of food, water, and sunlight gave him the best chance for creating an exceptional pumpkin. If you plant ten, the odds are that one will be much less and one will be much more than the other eight.

So you can aim for the "much more"—joy—and delight in the eight (contentment) with some certainty.

Life's Laws of Physics and, Yes, Taguchi's Loss Function.

In physics there's a law that says for every action there is an equal and opposite reaction. The slingshot gets pulled back, and it flies beyond the forks when you let go.

Sooner or later after the rubber bands quit bouncing, it settles, stopping and hanging in the middle. The starting point is the middle: halfway between the action and reaction.

For every action, there is an equal opposite reaction

The pendulum underneath the grandfather clock swings as far left as it does right, before settling in the middle when it stops. Let's see: so does a swing, a rocking chair, a rubber band and a yo-yo on the end of a string.

Now this is in the language of quality management. If it doesn't make sense, skip it and go to the next paragraph. If you understand it, it's downright poetic.

Taguchi's loss function demonstrates that the greater the deviation from target, the greater is the loss.

Loss—waste, deviation from the desired—is a function of variation. Imagine the profile of a bathtub—high walls, flat bottom. Hang a pendulum in the middle so you can watch its swing.

The wider the swing (the variation) the less time it spends on the bottom. A lot of energy is expended on that wide swing.

What would happen if that energy could be used to keep the swing narrower? If you could widen the bottom? Keep that swing narrow with a wider bottom?

A narrow swing means less variation. Less variation means more consistency. More consistency means more mastery

Slow down the swing!

A gardener built a four square foot planting bed. The gardener filled it with soil, found a packet of seeds, and scattered the entire packet in the bed.

As the seed sprouted, the gardener spent hours thinning the plants, no longer even sure of what they were.

Not sure of how many plants the bed would support and having thrown the seed packet away when the seeds were planted,

the gardener thinned too many plants and the harvest was far less than hoped for.

The next year, the gardener only planted half the packet in the bed. The harvest was still low.

Extreme Happiness:
Joy Is Juicy!

The third year, the gardener read the packet, and planted seeds according to the directions, with only three or four extra seeds, and the harvest was greater than in either of the previous two years.

The gardener reduced the variation deliberately, widened the bottom if you will, and had a higher volume and quality harvest.

The gardener might have gotten a little hung up with the idea: the gardener figured out how many seeds a 12x12 inch square would grow, and began to garden in square feet.

Whether he or she, all it took was tending that one square foot, making sure it was right for the number of plants it would grow.

No more big thickets of untended plants, too much food to harvest, the pain of thinning, or the need to weed.

It was small, more precise, and easier to tend.

Whether you're the gardener or the soil, part of hiking up Happy in your life is learning how to reduce the width of the swing. If you do that, you increase the control over variation.

And the gardener? Well, with less work because of using that square foot method, the gardener began to do something very different.

The gardener began to paint on the soil. The extra space? The areas in between those square foot blocks?

The gardener took flowers and planted the most gorgeous little plots of flowers—attracting bees and hummingbirds, and pleasing everyone's eyes who drove by.

The gardener smiled. The gardener was happier than ever with the small steps that had led, one after the other, to less labor and more joy.

Spinning like a top, arms outstretched

Face uplifted to the sky

The Light flowed into her upturned hand

And from the other palm to the ground

And the ground smiled in gratitude

Chapter Eight: How Do I Get Happier and Keep My Happy Up?

Get Physical: Move.

Sticks in the Mud Don't Smile.

Let's face it. The weight of Unhappy can drag you down—the weight of our uncertain times can too. Uncertainty, anxiety, and fear feed Unhappy. In the face of Unhappy, it's easy to quit moving.

Big movement—using your large muscles—helps you handle stress.

It's easy to zone in to the computer, the TV, the monitor—and to climb into that display. Sitting. Long Hours. This can create two things: (1) loss of physical conditioning and (2) a kind of emotional and mental numbness. If all you look at is the screen, it's a little hard to see the rest of the world.

Ironically, moving big—big muscle movement—can really help get your Happy up. Think about a day when you were so stressed you could barely breathe.

A few of your options for coping with that day:

- Stop at the local bar

- Get in the water (swim, kick, float, walk)
- Alter your chemistry with drugs
- Work out at the gym
- Bury yourself in TV
- Move dirt in the garden
- Play computer games
- Bake bread

Being still can be invisibility, meditative, or avoidance.

Every other one of these entries uses big muscles (arms and legs).

Using big muscles helps reduce the impact of stress (a key consequence of Unhappy) on the body. Ironically, they all require rhythmic motions. Rhythmic motion, such as rocking, can be very self-soothing.

The ones in between (drinking, drugging, zoning out on TV, computer games) are much more passive and tend to **bypass** rather than reduce stress and Unhappy.

The less you move, the "stiller" you are, the less likely it is you'll change expressions.

How do I Get Happier and Keep My Happy Up?

It's hypnotic to simply sit and go within, pull down the shades and live inside your mind or your monitor. Living "outside" of your body disinclines connection between emotions and facial expressions.

It's always a dance of balancing action and inaction.

Sticks stuck in the mud just stand. Motionless, without expression. Things to practice on days when you feel your Unhappy hiking up, or just stressed out, use movement to help you recover—like these activities:

- Walk, dance, run
- Swim, tread water, do water aerobics
- Garden, clear brush, mow, rake, sweep
- Participate in a team sport

What's Stuck in Your Craw is Stuck in Your Body.

Events are turned into memories when they occur, and memory is more than just the thoughts in words about what happened.

How do I Get Happier and Keep My Happy Up?

Memory has a feeling or emotional component, physical and sensory information as well, and may be continuous or broken up. Whatever is stuck, whether a videotape would show one version or another, needs to be moved (or flushed) on through.

Yoga is one of the best exercises for increasing Happy!

There are great practices that can help the body release things it is hanging on to in a kind and effective way:

- Massage, especially when you set an intention for the massage
- Yoga
- Acupuncture
- Body based therapies
- Trance dancing

Blessed are the Flexible for They Bend But Don't Break.

I've used the Y word a couple of times: yoga. If the word "yoga" makes you uncomfortable, substitute YMCA or your name.

You might find yoga classes at the local YMCA, and you can surely find yoga classes in your town, or a good DVD to work from.

Some senior citizens organizations offer yoga. Whatever the name of the activity is, it's about stretching, staying flexible, and increasing your balance.

Eat more dirt?

Symbolically, increasing your physical balance may make it more difficult to lose your emotional balance! What a kick in the shins to Unhappy that is.

Gardening has its own version of this, too. I need activity in my soil. Little bitty microbes, and worms, even flying bugs and beetles are all part of the life of the dirt.

Say, remember that I mentioned bacteria and dirt? Recent discoveries found specific bacteria in dirt relieve depression by increasing serotonin? Think I'm kidding? Google "dirt," and search within for "depression." Check it out.

At any rate, the dirt has a life too. And it needs activity for its' Happy to stay hiked up too! If your garden doesn't have enough activity in it, it grows pretty poor plants.

And while it can hardly have **too** much activity in terms of the good bugs and bacteria, if the activity is out of balance—too many bugs that need to be somewhere else, or a swarm moving through—it's just as bad. Ask my stick-topped beans visited by the grasshoppers.

Stay on your feet! Keep active! Stir up your molecules!

Here's another reason to get more physical. Fall prevention. Now I know this one down pat, as someone with really crummy knees. The thought of aging is scary enough when I think about it, or see someone whose body out-stepped their brain.

What's the price of falling? Did you know that one of the most common causes of incapacitation as people age is falling?

Why, it's just natural to lose hip strength, ankle and foot flexibility and balance as we age. Well, yes, of course. Pretty early on that flexible little body that loves to play and run gets molded to the seat of a chair, which is the first thing that helps us grow older too soon.

Yoga or stretching is really great at helping you stay on your feet longer and with more fun. It really, really helps with general flexibility, balance and gentle strengthening.

It can help reduce asthma, strengthen the grip, help your memory, cement new memories, reduces depression, helps with weight loss, and really helps your back? It does almost everything except plant the garlic.

Moving—using the large muscles—really helps reduce the knots, the stress, and the impact long and short term Unhappy has on you.

I want to point this little challenge out: while I believe counseling and therapy are really helpful, I did a lot of—years—of **talking** to try to address something that **happened**. It didn't get talked to or into me, but I sure tried to talk it out of me. Using only talking to try to address an experience leaves the stuff stuck in the body unaddressed.

Moving—adding movement to help me get the event unstuck—was one of the most helpful pieces of advice I took.

Try:

- Yoga
- Pilates
- Dance
- Massage
- Stretching like a cat

Get grounded—learn how to feel yourself and your feet on the ground. Play in the dirt.

Get Physical: Ground.

Mud-Pie Making Is More Than A Childhood Joy.

Most children get to make mud pies. If you set a toddler in front of a mud puddle where they can safely play, there will be splishing and splashing and some cute dirty Little Person is likely to "cook" with the mud.

I used to love to make mud pies in the edge of Grampy's garden. Fine ones they were, from the rich black soil not too far from the compost pile and the grey water line. That garden was just north of the old barn, and had once been a pasture. I'd squat down while Granny was hoeing or weeding, and make neat little pies of mud to offer her.

Granny wisely talked about how much more the birds needed the food, take an imaginary bite and then sent my mud pies flinging into the field pines. So much for the birds and the mud pies. She had a pretty good arm.

There is something basic about clay and dirt. Pottery, garden design and planting (you can do this), making mud pies as an adult, all that take your hand into direct contact with raw earth of some sort—all of these help reshape the self.

Working with dense clay in pottery and ceramics, like digging in the dirt, is so helpful!

Try taking a pottery class at the local recreation center, or buying some of that modeling material to play with.

Study your garden from the highest point around it and the angles from which it is seen. What kind of pattern can you make in it? What kind of picture can you draw?

Making mud pies is a simple frivolity anyone can access that boosts Happy. Try:

- Painting pottery at a "paint your own mug" place
- Drawing pictures in freshly dug dirt or sand

- Digging clay to make pottery
- Taking a pottery class Working with clay-based crafts (or the polymer-based bake-'em clays)

Gardening Bears Fruit.

Gardening is an absolute gift. To be able to make the soil sweeter for the plants, to select varieties with specific qualities, to watch them sprout, protect them from harm, support their growth—and then be rewarded with luscious fruits and vegetables—there really isn't much better than that.

The same thing is true when you're trying to jack your Happy up like that spider monkey "all jacked up on an energy drink." It's a process.

Horticulture is healing!

You prepare, select, sow, tend and also see the fruits of your efforts over time. Shoot, you could have a bumper crop of Happy and if you didn't recognize the plant, it'd just be a loss against what you expected in terms of your crop.

Used to be that the corporate world knew that any change they were implementing and wanted to adopt got dropped when they were about 2/3 of the way "there."

They'd work and show out and make like they were changing and all they did was rearrange trying to avoid things. And then sooner or later, they'd think everybody was "there" and the workplace returned to BAU—Business As Usual.

That corporate gardening for change stopped about.... 20% short in the season. And like my garden, when I just toss a packet of seeds down a row, that last 20% of the season is tough: all kinds of weeds have grown up. There's so much vegetation and crowding in that row where I tossed that packet of seeds that there's not much crop.

Plan and plant the garden in your life!

Want fruit? Know what kind of fruit you want, what kind of change you want to see in your life? How the Happy looks? Plant and tend the seeds for that fruit—avoid overcrowding while you learn the ins and outs of the plant and its needs.

Now, let me tell you. When I just tossed a packet of seeds down a crookedy row, it was chaos. Kind of like when I started doing some counseling and could say "I want to get better."

How do I Get Happier and Keep My Happy Up?

As I began to practice a much more precise form of gardening—the square foot method—I got phenomenal results. The same was true as I decided I'd be better of to define what "better" meant.

The same way getting a little (or a lot) more precise about what different plants needed (and giving it to them) really boosted my crop, getting clearer about how I'd know if I was hanging out in Happy made getting there a lot easier.

Feel the grass and the earth beneath your bare feet.

Treat yourself as a garden—plan what you want in your life, where, and for what reason. While you're at it, grow some of your own food—you'll be healthier, and chances are, happier.

Try these:

- Plant flowers
- Grow vegetables
- Start a community garden or a Victory Garden Plant a tree
- Put in a new mailbox post Volunteer at the local park
- Learn how to garden
- Make a compost pile

How do I Get Happier and Keep My Happy Up?

- Eat local foods
- Pick at a pick-your-own farm
- Volunteer at a community garden
- Create a community garden

Barefoot and Birthing Yourself.

When's the last time your feet touched bare earth? Did you feel it when they did? You know: did you really feel the earth and how far beneath your feet it goes?

Walking means getting one foot off the ground..

There is something fundamental about the connection between our feet and the earth. It drains "stuff" out, it fills us up, and is amazing—when we stop and experience it.

I don't remember going barefoot outside, although I know once I was at the creek, my socks and shoes had to come off. They had to be on, clean(ish) and dry when I got home.

Maybe it was my knees, and somehow wearing shoes was supposed to keep them from getting any worse? Who knows! The long and short of it is that the only callous on either foot is on the inside edge of my big toe, from walking a little funny. Never have had tough feet.

When I lived in Las Vegas ever so briefly, I saw what people called "desert feet" and I swear it looked like gnarly pine on the bottom of those people's feet. I understood (which I never had before) why people sanded off calluses.

We come into this world barefoot, with tender feet. We spend the first years of our lives growing and learning how to stand on those feet, use them for walking, running, skipping, jumping, hopping, digging, all kinds of things. Until we don shoes, they are in direct contact with whatever we walk on.

Take your shoes off, get in touch, let the dirt help you find Happy. Or Happy(er). Try these:

- Take your shoes off in a grassy spot
- Put your bare feet on the ground, feel each blade of grass on the soles of your feet
- Feel the earth. Feel the connection between the two, what it feels like.

Since it's just a feeling, all you have to do is:

- Let it in, and let it go through: feel from the soles of your feet,up through your body, up through your spine
- Then feel the feeling leaving your body through the top of your head or the ends of your fingers

You can practice letting the feeling stay, too, or holding it in just one place.

Rate your Happy and re-rate the level every so often—see how you're doing.

- Let your feet rest in warm sand, cool freshly dug dirt
- Plant them in the flower or herb bed on top of soothing chamomile plants, velvety pansies, piney rosemary
- Walk on the ground instead of concrete and pavement

Walking Requires One Foot on the Ground.

No kidding. Think about it. You lift one foot, place it in front of you on the ground as you begin to lift the other foot.

Forward motion only occurs if one foot is placed in front of the other foot repeatedly. One foot is always on the ground.

You have two feet on the ground, heel to toe, you're standing still. Planted. Sometimes that's a good thing, and sometimes it reflects being stuck ,stuck, stuck.

Balance between stability and [illegible]

The benefit of stability weighed down by the risk of stagnation. When Happy requires action, standing still isn't very helpful. When Happy requires reflection and simply experiencing, standing still is what's called for.

So what's the importance of keeping **one** foot on the ground? Could it be that with the balance between air and earth there might be more possibility?

What happens to plants that don't or can't reach for the sky? Even when they are root vegetables, they need to reach up and out to feed what's below.

How do I Get Happier and Keep My Happy Up?

If you have two feet on the ground, how easy is it to move when you need to? How hard is it to know what's next or to be really connected when both feet are off the ground?

Being grounded, or connected with your self (mind, body, feelings, spirit) is so valuable! With **one** foot on the ground, you ground with the earth while the other foot keeps you from getting stuck.

Grounding in the earth helps us remember who we are.

Which foot do you put forward first? Here are some ways to play:

- Stand on one foot for as long as you can
- increase the time
- Relax while standing on one foot

Standing on one foot, imagine the energy cycling from the foot on the ground up one side and down the other, out the raised foot and then into the earth

- Walk aware of what your feet are doing
- Start with the opposite foot

- Pay attention to how these actions feel
- Compare your Happy **before** to **after** them

The Potter Molds The Clay.

How you work with this in terms of hiking up your Happy is up to you.

Mold and be molded.

Do you believe you are a "Created creature," brought into being by that which we call G-d (spelled to respect traditions where the name is so sacred the "o" is omitted)?

If so, when you read "the potter molds the clay" you may think in the direction of a personalized G-d that takes a particular and personal interest in us.

Perhaps you think, "my parents made me what I am" or "I changed to make my spouse happy." This depends entirely on how you define "potter" and what you think of when you think about "clay."

When the Potter is something or someone greater, wiser, older, more in charge and with more power than you have, it's dangerous to be "clay."

How do I Get Happier and Keep My Happy Up?

Why are bubbles so much fun? How can they help hike up your Happy?

- They're light and airy
- They're beautiful
- They capture the imagination
- They can symbolically carry thoughts and feelings away
- They can make you laugh

A lot of trust is required to let yourself be molded. Of course, as a Little Person with minimal experience you trusted anyone who cared for you until you learned otherwise (if you did).

What happens when you consider yourself the Potter, too? As an adult, and as someone curious about this whole idea of Getting Happier, you have the ability to mold clay, too.

Every time you interact with someone else, you are molding them as they mold you—shared creation. Every time you interact with yourself, this too is shared creation, self-molding.

Self-molding is as important as being molded by others. Of course, your skill as a sculptor of the self is developed when you are a Little Person.

Remember: this is about Getting Happier, so think of this model as able to express emotions, thoughts, needs and wants.

This is about more than those thunder thighs you might have developed sitting still!

- How will you mold your clay?
- When you think of people you consider as having "big Happy" what do they do that lets you see Happy?
- What thought do you have that is constantly self-critical?
- How does that thought serve you?
- What would happen if you changed it?
- How does sitting still, not moving help you?

Get Physical: Fly.

Kites Carry Life.

You know why kites are so important in American history? Get curious!

Look up Ben Franklin and kites. He used a kite to prove electricity existed, and he also used a kite to be pulled along while floating in water.

Kites may have originated in the South Sea Islands, where people used them to fish. Now that's a direct connection to life.

In China, the first kites lifted people for military purposes. Protecting yourself or defending against an enemy is life-bringing.

Go fly a kite.

In India, the holiday Uttarayan marks the day when the sun begins to travel northward. It is the day that winter begins to decline. As celebrated in one city of India, it is the time to watch in ceaseless amazement. From competitions to prayers written on them to lift them skyward, kites play a central role.

In Oaxaca, kites lift the souls on the Day of the Dead. This is a day to pray for and remember family and friends who have died.

The Maori people of New Zealand used kites to celebrate their belief that birds could carry messages between people and the gods. Their god Rehua is depicted as a bird, and is considered to be the ancestor of all kites.

Kites carry life, and there is nothing as exhilarating as flying them. Ever have a dream about flying? Check out what the dream interpreters say about it.

Watch for messages in all that you see.

How do kites and kite flying relate to Getting Happier? Consider these:

- When's the last time you flew a kite?
- Can you identify five things about your life you'd like a kite to carry skyward?
- Where do people fly kites in your city or area?
- How else did you "fly" as a child or want to "fly"?
- Are there swing sets in the parks large enough for you to swing on?
- Could you para-sail or para-glide? Where?

- What meaning could you attach to activities involving air that would help you hike up your Happy?
- How can you use air to help you release upward bits and pieces of Unhappy and bring downward drafts of contentment?

Fireflies Light the Night.

Watch the fireflies and the stars.

When I was young, I guess just about out of high school or early in college, I took off and rode up to Brown Mountain.

Now if North Carolina's Brown Mountain is new to you, look it up. It's up off of Highway 181, well past the old Morganton radio tower everybody used to climb when they got drunk

You go on past St. Mary's at Quaker Meadows, the little Episcopal Church on the right, then up the mountain past the road to Brown Mountain Beach and Wilson's Gorge.

Sooner or later you come to a dirt pull-off. There ot is on the right: a long, rectangular gravel parking lot with a boulder on the uphill end perched as if to roll at any minute.

With that boulder on you left, you look out just in front of you—and there you see a long, loaf-like mountain with a smooth and even crest. It sits down, not the furthest out. To me, it was as if there were a field of pines like a flank up to its crest. You could see right down on top of those trees.

I parked on that lot, with that boulder to my left (and therefore uphill). It was dusk, and not too long after it got dark, there they were: the Brown Mountain Lights. Little lights, then bigger ones—coming up off Brown Mountain. It was eerie. I took off.

Went back a few weeks later. Went back again when I lived back there from 1999 through 2003. Took care of my Stepdad in those years, and stayed after he passed (died).

I'd had a hard day doing a little planting in my first garden, a little bitty one at my growing-up place. I found so many marbles in that garden I decided if I ever wrote an autobiographical piece I'd have to call it "Finding My Marbles."

A ride seemed like a good idea. I ambled along the Catawba River wishing I owned a little river bottom land because it is so rich and fertile.

Turned right off Highway 18 onto Highway 181 North. Passed the radio tower. The church.

Pulled off not at my usual place but the next one up—you could sometimes see the Lights from there.

Look for the miraculous.

Not tonight. What I **could** see were lightning bugs or fireflies, the orange with the black striped edge wing. They began tentatively sending out their messages from the tree beside my car and started their evening chat.

Pretty soon the wide slope of trees was blinking and then it went dark—only to start up again after what felt like an eternity.

And the fireflies looked to me like they were little Ethel Mermans, all synchronized in this vast airy performance.

It was the only time I ever saw that, and every time even one of those newer black fireflies with the red head lights up, I remember what I saw and the absolute awe and wonder. Those little glowing bugs lit up the night, tuned up and synched up and there they went.

Now there's been some study done on "synchronized fireflies" in the US and up in Elkmont TN.. This wasn't Elkmont, and yet I say that what I saw looked synchronized.

Truthfully, it doesn't really matter: what I saw was incredible, it looked like this to me, and if someone else were to say "not so," I think I'd hang on to the memory anyhow.

Things to do that help you move and engage aspects of flight:

- Research "fireflies" to find out more about them
- If you live in an area they populate, begin to watch for them in June (if not, there are some interesting videos of fire flies on the Internet).

- Do you ever watch birds as they fly, land, feed? If not, try it
- Are there bird feeders by your windows where you can see flight?
- Could you grow sunflowers in view of your windows for the birds?
- Do you have any outside lights you can place somewhere so they will twinkle softly?

Love the birds.

Think about the mid-summer experience of sitting in a yard or a clearing waiting for fire flies to start rising from the ground.

What does it look, feel, smell, like? Is it pleasant (it is for me!)? If so, remember it.

Trance Out

There was a child who grew up spending every waking minute buried in a book or a TV. Over time, the TV gave way to computer and console games. The books gave way to the internet. The child seldom knew daylight from dark.

Another played and ran and spent every minute outside playing make believe with cousins.

The day passed so quickly they lost track of time, and sometimes where they were until the looked up and sighted the Big Pine in the forest behind the sawdust pile where the land had been timbered.

Be conscious about how you use dissociation or trance.

An adult sits behind a desk, working, immersed in a new project. Lunch passes. Mid-afternoon goes by.

Dark falls, and no one has seen the adult's face.

When maintenance clicks off the lights, there is a startled flurry. My how time flies when you're having... fun? Call it what you want, it's a form of self-hypnosis.

I get up, feed the cat, and head for the garden coffee in hand. I look at the plants, tug on a few stalks of the plants, tug on a few stalks of sprouted oat straw. I piddle around, do this and that, and grub in the dirt.

Before I know it, it's not 715 in the morning, it's 10am.

How do I Get Happier and Keep My Happy Up?

What do all these have in common?

They all represent forms of socially acceptable trance states—of disconnecting from some aspect of experience.

Dissociation is part and parcel of everyday life. Some of it we need, some we could change.

How do you get outside of yourself in ways that are intentional and useful, giving your mind a break?

Do something silly and light.

- Get absorbed in a book
- Take up walking or running, working towards "runner's high"
- Do yoga or some form of exercise that requires full focus
- Engage in formal meditation
- Find a repetitive spiritual practice, like praying with beads or reminders of some sort
- Perform manual (safer) repetitive labor
- Hum (which also seems to help your sinuses!)

- Pay attention to how spaced out you get the next time you are driving or flying
- Make a bubble mill (http://family.go.com/entertainment/craft-ff-25254-bubble-mill-t/)! Can you imagine?

Get Physical: Act.

Make a Plan, Act on It, Finish Your Incompletes.

All the incompletes drag you down.

You may not finish what you set out to do. You surely won't finish anything you don't start.

How many things have you promised to do, agreed to start, set out to try—and they're left dangling like an old brogan tossed over a telephone line?

Here's the challenge: all those incompletes you have—things you say you'll do, things you meant to do, things you—oh, you get it.

They're like fishing line that we toss out and leave dangling, becoming huge balls of string that we tote everywhere we go.

They take energy to think about, regret, recoup, and rekindle.

It's easy to over-commit and under-do.

And when your Unhappy trumps your Happy, it's easy to either do nothing, or go frantic to try to shift things around!

The most important action you can take in getting happier is decide you'd like to and pay attention as you go forward:

Make sure your commitment and activity match.

- Listen to your thoughts, and hike up the happy in them
- Square your shoulders, put some bounce in your step, and walk with your head up—as if you have meaning in life
- Spend time outdoors feeling the sun, wind, and air on your face
- Clean up the incompletes left dangling and cut back on over-committing and under-doing

- Decide, every day, to Hike Up Your Happy
- Make an appointment with yourself at least twice a year.
- Think about the things you started, the things you said you'd do and didn't.

Treat your mind like a wandering sheep. Herd it.

Make a list, and decide how to clean these up: complete the incompletes and stand back! Because the energy you free up is amazing.

It's like breaking up good rich soil that's been compacted: it wants to breathe, to feel air and see sun.

You can hardly grow anything well on compacted soil, even when it's fabulous dirt.

Make Mental Matter: Choose.

Shepherd Your Mind.

Oh my. Bless my little mind, it's been a strained brain for a long time, and even before then, it wandered. I'm sure.

How do I Get Happier and Keep My Happy Up?

I used to have a lot of trouble with managing my mind for one reason or another. Now it seems to be from sheer brain fatigue and age!

I've even read something about what long hours in front of a computer do to fatigue the brain. I surely spend them. What to do?

Strive for more and longer periods of balance.

Every year, I look at the garden. I remember the patterns of where things were last year.

I think about what needs to be rotated, where the companion plants need to go.

In other words, I've formed a pattern. And there will probably come a time when I form another one about the garden because change will be necessary for one reason or another. Did I mention I think growing artichokes in Nashville could be fun?

Since I was born, my brain has learned patterns of attentiveness, inattentiveness, association and dissociation—and each time I learn a new one, it changes my brain!

Literally: what we repeat build specific patterns of brain activity. The more we repeat them, the more stable they become (OK, I'm simplifying it a lot here).

I think a lot of the scatterbrained -ness of today's time is related to the attention span we develop. The fact that our world does not require or encourage us in focusing on one idea at a time for a period of time. Few people actually sit and read, and think about what they read or try to reason something out. Few of us follow a thought to its end.

Most people (me, too!) are content to zone out, in front of a TV or computer, or to get so thoroughly absorbed (associated) in an activity that they lose focus on everything else

Yet our brains learn that attention spans should be the length of time of a typical media clip, ranging from 30 seconds to twenty minutes.

Attention span and the ability to focus as well as think effectively will profoundly influence our ability to shepherd and manage our thoughts. If we can't sit still and focus long enough to identify them, we probably can't do anything with them. Point made.

Ever take a seat on the edge of your mind and watch or listen to your thoughts? Do you ever finish your own internal conversations? How easy is it for you to catch yourself thinking something and change the thought?

It really is possible to become more conscious of what you think, feel and do—and to begin to train your mind to be more effective, to attend longer and with greater direction.

Do you practice changing your thoughts deliberately, or thinking a particular thought over and over? Singing the same song over and over again can be a good thing when the song carries messages that help you hike up Happy.

Try any of these things! They help you change your mind (literally).

And there are great brain training games online, some of which are free. I personally like www.lumosity.com and www.mindhabits.com. They help me when I need to focus, distract, or redirect my mind.

Other computer games that help you get that brain back in shape? www.happyneuron.com, www.mindfit.com. Short on cash? Take the free demos. Even they will help—then figure out which one is for you, and go from there.

Sincere kindness to yourself is a good thing.

There's evidence now, that computer games for training the brain do some good.

So please start down that road only if you **really** want to get happier, part of which is learning to shepherd your thoughts and feelings so they go where you want them to go. Not where every marketer, media maven, and person who has a little influence wants them to.

Seriously. It takes time, practice and more practice. It kind of reminds me of training a dog, except I'm the trainer and the b.. uh, dog.

Compassion for Your Thoughts.

Now this could sound a little odd, and I'm convinced it's true. Shepherding your mind takes having compassion for your thoughts.

In other words, it's back to those flies: you catch more with honey (compassion) than you do with vinegar (condemnation). It takes practice to be more compassionate to you.

Compassion is a high form of love.

Learning compassion for yourself is like getting in shape (and committing to grow your own food). Once you start, it's important to keep it up, and to periodically change up what you do to keep it fresh.

You also want to pay attention to the relationships between your thoughts, actions, and the outcomes.

I know you talk to yourself. I do. I know everyone does—and that most of the time we're pretty mean to us!

What's your self-talk like? If you're like a lot of people I know, you've got a lot of insults and tacky things you say to yourself when you don't live up to your expectations, or when you do something you think is "dumb" or "stupid."

Those comments roll right to the big Unhappy Hole. They do. I know because I still unpack a few now and then and have to wrestle them to the ground.

As unruly as a Kudzu vine on steroids, fast-growing, aggressive, the self-condemning thoughts are delighted to take over whatever and wherever they can.

Good news, bad news. The good news? Yes, you can indeed change the conversation. This is, I think, very good news. The bad news is it takes practice, and the meaner you are to you, the longer it takes.

Truly.

Now this is once again different from being phony-nice to yourself. It's different from being crazy in drag. It's different from being icky-pooey sweet-ums every moment, even if you wish. you could do something different. Isn't it true?

We had this conversation earlier, and I'm still convinced in spite of the tantrums I've been seeing it's so.

There's just no evidence that 90% of us (the middle of that Bell Curve and one half of the outliers) wake and consciously decide to be jerks to everyone else—and ourselves.

Acting like you are an automatic (insert your own word for rear end here) kicker, tripping your own trigger to boot yourself in the behind over and over again doesn't help you learn very much.

It's a little like me going out in my garden and ripping up the whole thing because one row isn't right, replanting, seeing I still have a crooked row, and ripping it up again and replanting—and then wondering a couple of months down the road why there's no harvest! Sounds like how I used to (and still sometimes do) beat myself up verbally—and set up getting beat up by others.

What could I do different?

Let's see. I could have...laughed and let the row be crooked... moved only a few of the plants to straighten the row a little... found a few plants and added to the row to make it look deliberate.

I could have accepted the fact that crooked rows really are fine. Fine. The plants weren't the least bit disturbed by their circumstances.

All of the judgments I passed affected what I wanted—a good harvest—negatively. They made me doubt my own abilities. I felt guilty and had a shame attack (if you've ever had one, you know it).

In my experience, this is a better pattern of self-talk among those parts of me hunkered down in the interior—this is all self-talk:

Scenario 1

Ouizie: OK, this fear I'm feeling may be bigger than the situation is.

Grump: NO IT'S NOT—WE'RE GOING TO DIE!!!

Ouizie: I can tell I'm feeling really scared.

Grump: SCARED MY A**! WE'RE GONNA DIE!!!

Ouizie: How many people have been in the same situation? Lots. Did they die? No. Were they frightened? Yes. Did they make it through? Yes, some more gracefully than others.

Grump: WE'RE GONNA DIE.

Ouizie: I know you're frightened—how can I help you feel safer?

Grump: Are you SURE we're not gonna die?

Ouizie: I'm sure.

Scenario 2

Grump: Oh no. I really screwed that one up. Can you believe it? I knew I would screw that up. I should have never tried. 30 years in this and I miss a line and freeze. I'm over the hill. I am.

Ouizie: OK, let's listen to the feedback we got—a lot of people said well done, and she said the team did great. Has she sugarcoated anything before? No.

Grump: I knew I was too old and burned out for this. I should have never tried. Never. How stupid can I be!

Ouizie: Easy does it—of course I feel embarrassed and stupid, and the fact is, she liked what we did. So maybe this is just one where feelings and facts are a mismatch.

Grump: Hmph. I just can't believe she liked it.

Ouizie: Well, she has a history of speaking her mind just like you do—so you both have that in common. I doubt either one of you is good at lying...

Grump: We'll never live it down!

Ouizie: Is this going to be important to me ten years from now? Who will remember today ten years from now?

Grump: OMG. Pollyanna strikes again. Who CARES about ten years, I can't stand it NOW.

Ouizie: Let's go take a walk. That'll help. We'll just go fast around the driveway once.

All of these are kinder, more compassionate responses. They're the things I say to myself. I practice them as much as I can.

I'm telling you, it's like training a wire haired Fox Terrier—you might even try clicker training in your house if there's another set of opposable digits (cats can't help with clicker training and neither can dogs).

Yes, you are the source and sum of your choices.

The self-contempt that makes it hard to cope with these trying times is best soothed with compassion.

It's the most basic thing I can offer myself.

What might happen if you talked to yourself in a compassionate instead of condemning way? Ok, so you already do—what might happen if you increased the frequency, paid attention to the practice?

You're the only one who can raise you the way you think children should have been raised. You're the only person who will truly be there for you when the stuff hits the fan (if everyone else falls away).

Expect it to take a while, and to need to keep the practice up—and when you forget how, just turn to the new way as soon as you remember—without fuss, or making a big to-do.

The sum of our choices. That's what we all are. So the more you choose in the direction of the things that really matter—like less stress, feeling better, and trumping Unhappy— the more you are redirecting your life to Happy.

Shepherd your thoughts. They're yours, own them, guide them, and give them the map.

Have compassion for your thoughts. They represent different parts of you all responding to the same event.

Build yourself up—cut you a little slack when Grump starts to trump Ouizie. Instead of beating up on Ouizie, soothe Grump.

Tend your mind with the same longing a rabbit has for a lettuce bed. Coach yourself as if it meant you'd surely end up on the winningest sports team in history. Treat it like a prize pup with the potential to win the Westminster Kennel Club (that's a BIG dog show).

Engage the Emotional.

Increase Your Feelings Vocabulary

Feeling? I'm feeling? I used to just plant tomatoes and sweet potatoes. That was all. Likewise, I felt "good" or "bad." They were red and yellow, and I felt good or bad.

I had a pretty limited selection in the outer and the inner garden. No doubt about it. I hardly knew when I felt anything—and I surely didn't have a big vocabulary for the occasion!

Did you know there are purple tomatoes? White tomatoes? Sweet ones? Tomatoes so acid they pucker you up? Yellow and striped ones? Tomatoes with no seeds and some with thin skins?

Some shaped like pears, some round, and some gnarly? Even ones that are so dark they are called "black" and so light they are called "white."

Same with potatoes. Even in the sweet potato family, there are pink, orange, yellow, white ones?

Some with really smooth and some with fibrous starchy texture? Different leaves and blossoms—all sweet potatoes.

Same with emotions. I think the big three are fear, love, and pleasure. Bad, good, and good—all three with serious danger attached to them if you don't know what to do with them.

How's your vocabulary for feelings? How about your **recognition** of when your feeling states change? Labels for the from and to?

Use Your Feelings Vocabulary

Expand your emotional repertory.

You can utilize what you know about. The more you are aware that you do feel, and can identify when you feel, the more you have an opportunity to explore and label what you do feel. With that, you can choose what to do with those feelings more and more often.

This is powerful.

We express our feelings very freely when we are on the BBEY train. In the uterus, we have the chemical experience our mother has.

I am clueless about what our consciousness of emotion in utero is.

And I know we don't have filters on expressions or much differentiation among them at first.

I do know that whatever the limits of our environment is in modeling the expression of a feeling will be our limits. Until and unless we do something conscious about it.

The broader your emotional palette—just like the greater the variety of plants in your garden—the richer your experience of life.

Two words or twenty? Which offers more choices, more options, more personal power? Fear, love, pleasure—or terror, trembling, fright, fear, anxiety; passion, ardor, devotion, love, appreciation, acceptance; ecstasy, joy, delight, pleasure, contentment?

Here are questions to ask and explore:

- How can you find out about more names of feelings and what they are like?

- How can you practice feeling different feelings in a safe way?
- What can you do to enlarge the range of your emotions?
- What tools, such as a thesaurus, might help you?

Separate feelings and facts. Feel the feelings, act on facts.

- Who do you think has a broader range and better management of emotions than you do? (In other words, who is your role model?)
- Can you ask them about their feelings? (Remember—they may never have stepped back to look either!)

Emotional literacy is an important part of getting happier. Have you ever googled "emotional intelligence"? Try it!

Emotional intelligence is something you can learn no matter how booksmart you are!

Kind of like your mind, your feelings need some help—from you. The first thing you need to help them with is to recognize they're there!

OK. You see them. You acknowledge them, and they treat you like they're the big dog on the block and all you are is a fire hydrant.

Manage and Master Your Feelings

Like your thoughts, shepherd them and have compassion for your feelings. I know, I know it's like having a two year old throwing a temper tantrum in the grocery store: who wants to face that?! Just get it to shut up and go away (I mean, embarrassing!).

Remember those scenes between Ouizie and Grump? How Ouizie was, well, grounded and respectful and supportive of Grump? That's the style to practice—and here's a scene about how challenging it can be.

Scenario 3

Grump: How stupid. I can't believe how stupid I am. They were right: I should have never been born.

Ouizie: What a screw-up! I shot myself in the foot again. Go figure.

Grump: Yeah, right. Stupid. Screw up. Self-destructive—now there's one!

Ouizie: Yeah, I'm like a coyote gnawing on my own leg.

Treat your emotions as messengers—what information do they bring you?

Grump: You should be so lucky! Death would come faster then at least.

Ouizie: There's no point. Wait a minute—there's no point: can I turn that feeling around? It's like a rock in the pit of my stomach. I wonder if I could move it?

Grump: GRRRRRRRR!!! You can't get anything right!

Ouizie: Probably not—so I'm going to mess up again: if it's all my fault, I'm at least going to have a good time. I can choose that much.

Grump: Oh yeah. Like you know what a good time is.

How do I Get Happier and Keep My Happy Up?

Ouizie: I know that I can look at this any way I want to. I can frame it as the same old stuff, or as another experience I can learn from. If I learn the right things, maybe I can quit shooting myself in the foot so much!

Make a way for you to remind yourself that all the feelings bring you some form of information. Increase the range of your emotional library. And when strong feelings come up, manage them so you can keep all your options open.

You can get happier, no matter how happy you are.

I know that life can stress you to the edge where you hold on like a squirrel on a greased bird feeder pole

I know you can go from rags to riches and back faster than a frog catches a fly.

I know your heart can break in a million pieces. I know.

I know that you can be so crushed, wounded, or content that there seems to be no change you need (or can tolerate).

And I know that getting out of that big old Unhappy hole and learning to live in Happy is a journey.

I also know that begin Happy and working to change the Happy set point is hard work.

Even when you get happy, and can see Happy in your life, you can still get happier.

It's a great journey. And it's a journey of real importance in our times: the best way we can begin to create and pass on a desirable virus that makes us all more resilient when times get tough.

Of course, your Happy is up to you. Wherever you are in relationship to Happy, you can always... get happier.

Getting happier is the mandate of our times and the choice of our lives!

Local Ad in the Cosmic Times, written just for you:

Happiness is up for grabs, get yours today.

Visit us on the Web!

At www.gettinghappier, you can:

- *Become part of the Getting Happier community*
- *Sign up for our e-zine*
- *Buy Elizabeth Power's other books, DVDs, and spoken word audio*
- *Buy products featuring Ouize and Grump*
- *Follow our great links to other resources*
- *Download FREE articles*
- *Find out more out Getting Happier Seminars*
- *Learn more about us*

www.gettinghappier.com

Life gets better, life gets worse—
either way,
you can always get happier!

www.ingramcontent.com/pod-product-compliance
Lightning Source LLC
LaVergne TN
LVHW090952080826
845145LV00003B/978

* 9 7 8 1 8 8 3 3 0 7 0 8 0 *